FIREHOUSE FOOD

FIREHOUSE FOOD

COOKING WITH SAN FRANCISCO'S FIREFIGHTERS

BY **George Dolese** & **Steve Siegelman**

PHOTOGRAPHS BY **Paul Moore**

CHRONICLE BOOKS

SAN FRANCISCO

To San Francisco's Firefighters,

who understand the sustaining power of a nice hot meal.

Library of Congress Cataloging-in-Publication Data:
Dolese, George.
    Firehouse food : cooking with San Francisco's firefighters / by George Dolese & Steve Siegelman; photographs by Paul Moore.
        p. cm.
        ISBN 0-8118-3988-5 (pbk.)
1. Cookery. 2. San Francisco (Calif.). Fire Dept. I. Siegelman, Stephen. II. Title.
TX714 .D618 2003
641.5—dc21
        2002151454

Manufactured in Singapore.
Food and prop styling by George Dolese
Design by Catherine Jacobes

Distributed in Canada by Raincoast Books
9050 Shaughnessy Street
Vancouver, British Columbia V6P 6E5

10 9 8 7 6 5 4 3

Chronicle Books LLC
85 Second Street
San Francisco, California 94105
www.chroniclebooks.com

I want to express my deepest thanks to the crews of all the stations in which I photographed. Wherever I showed up, I was given free access and felt welcome and well fed. This book is the result of a few people all giving more than what is typical or expected. Without that attitude it wouldn't have been possible. Thanks to the New Lab for donating their high-quality digital prints and to Catherine Jacobes for editing more than 1,000 shots and for her great design.
                                                                    —Paul Moore

ACKNOWLEDGMENTS

Right from our first meeting, the San Francisco Fire Department rolled up its doors for us and made us feel welcome. We thank SFFD Chief Mario Trevino for his enthusiastic support of this project and for his heartfelt foreword. And we're grateful to Public Information Officer Pete Howes, who put us in touch with the people and information we needed every step of the way, and to Administrative Lt. Nicol Juratovac at Headquarters, whose organization and efficiency were invaluable in setting up firehouse visits, interviews, and photo shoots.

Early on in the project, Pete Howes asked firefighter Karen Kerr to be our day-to-day contact, and she quickly rose to the rank of "guardian angel." Karen, thanks for your hard work, your encouragement, and most of all the cheerful make-it-happen attitude you bring to everything you do.

As we collected hundreds of recipes, Elisabet Der Nederlanden spent many long days testing them and assisting with the styling of the food photos. Thanks, Elisabet, for your calming presence, your great palate, your attention to detail, and your sense of humor, even on the third and fourth rounds.

Tina Salter saved the day by testing several recipes during the final crunch. Thank you, Tina, as always, for your warmhearted dedication to getting it right and making it tasty.

We thank the staff at Chronicle Books—especially Bill LeBlond, Ben Shaykin, and Amy Treadwell—for sharing our vision from the start, and copy editor Rebecca Pepper for her thorough and helpful input.

Thanks to La Rocca Seafood, Liguria Bakery, H&E Noodle Factory, and Mary and Ray Lopez for participating in photo sessions, and Leslie Busch for first steering George to the 1965 *San Francisco Firehouse Favorites* cookbook.

Thank you Martin Lewis for keeping the home fires burning; and Philip, Ellen, and Peter Siegelman for testing, tasting, and talking it through.

Paul Moore's photos perfectly capture the spontaneity and camaraderie of cooking and eating in the firehouses of San Francisco, and Catherine Jacobes's design brings that experience home with just the right balance of simplicity and style. Thanks to you both for making it fun and keeping it real.

And finally, we thank the firefighters of San Francisco who shared their recipes, their stories, and their meals with us. We wish we had the space in these pages to include every recipe you submitted, and we're grateful to you all for the time and thought you put into your contributions. As heroes and role models, you have a lot to be proud of. We hope this book makes you even prouder.

—George Dolese and Steve Siegelman

TABLE OF CONTENTS

FOREWORD	8
INTRODUCTION	13
SALADS & SOUPS	**31**
MAIN DISHES	**63**
SIDES	**153**
DESSERTS	**183**
INDEX	217
MENU PLANNER	222
TABLE OF EQUIVALENTS	224

FOREWORD

Mario H. Trevino | Chief, San Francisco Fire Department

It's been many years since a book was written to commemorate the recipes and dining traditions of the San Francisco Fire Department, and, in my estimation, there has never been a more appropriate time than the present for a cookbook with a fire department theme.

Situated as it is on the beautiful and bountiful Pacific Ocean, San Francisco is renowned as the home of some of the finest restaurants in the world. Every visitor leaves with memories of outstanding meals that reflect a cosmopolitan city, rich with a diversity that rivals the great metropolises of the world. However, one of the best-kept secrets of the "City," as it's called by locals, is a long-standing epicurean tradition in the many historic firehouses that dot the urban landscape.

San Francisco firefighters come in all shapes, sizes, backgrounds, and lifestyles. Competition for a spot in the department is fierce, and that competition continues throughout the decades that span a firefighter's career. But while the members of the SFFD may not always agree during their 24-hour shifts, dinnertime has always been an oasis. It's a time when everyone sits down at the table and shares a meal over lively conversation. The pressure to please "the house" is palpable and not to be taken lightly; the cook needs to make it good, and make a lot of it.

The same strong hands that take on the roughest challenges a big city can dish out can also put the finishing touches on a world-class meal to satisfy the biggest appetites and the most discriminating palates.

My personal favorite time to spend with the firefighters and officers is at the end of the business day, when I can visit any station around the City and sample the feast that awaits the members. Whether it's the Sunset, the Fillmore, Fisherman's Wharf, or Nob Hill, I know that a wonderful meal invariably awaits me and that the brave men and women who risk their lives on a daily basis have prepared it with single-minded enthusiasm.

Please enjoy your tour through the dining experiences of the San Francisco Fire Department and know that some of the proceeds of this book are being generously donated to the SFFD Surviving Families Fund.

Bon appétit!

Surviving Families Fund

The authors will donate a portion of the proceeds from the sale of this book to the Surviving Families Fund of San Francisco Firefighters Local 798, which provides financial support to the families of the city's fallen firefighters.

For more information about the fund, please contact Local 798 at (415) 621-7103.

INTRODUCTION

"I don't mind rushing into a burning building," says Chase Wilson with a grin, as she carefully sears a poblano chile over the flame of a gas range. "It's putting dinner on the table for 14 people that gets my adrenaline going. That's definitely the scariest part of the job."

Chase, now in her third year as a San Francisco firefighter, is kidding, of course. But not entirely. When her monthly cooking shift comes up, she's all business—her personal recipe notebook at the ready, her shopping list in order, the prep assignments doled out to anyone with time on their hands.

As she watches the chile blister and blacken, she runs through tonight's menu. There's a Mexican-style salad with a cilantro–sour cream dressing, slow-simmered pork in mole sauce, scratch-made black beans, Mexican red rice, and fresh warm flour tortillas. And for dessert, she's persuaded one of her colleagues to make a double batch of pineapple upside-down cake.

For some firefighters, kitchen duty can be fun. For others, it's a chore. Some see it as a chance to give something special to people they care about. And there are those—especially the first-year "probies"—who find it a little intimidating. But whatever else it may be, firehouse cooking is never taken lightly, and it is never just about feeding people.

"I don't mind rushing into a burning building. It's putting dinner on the table for 14 people that gets my adrenaline going. That's definitely the scariest part of the job."

After all, a firehouse isn't simply a municipal institution—a garage for engines and equipment. It's a house. And a house is a place where a family lives.

Sure, it's a family of adults, some of whom may have just met each other. But it's also a family that shares a common desire to help people in trouble—a family that faces the possibility of unimaginable danger together every day. For a family like that, meals mean a lot. There's no grabbing a yogurt for lunch or skipping dinner. Every day of the year at noon and 7:00 P.M., the firehouse family sits down around a single table. And at least once a day, if not twice, what they sit down to is an enormous, piping hot, deeply satisfying, home-cooked, special-occasion meal.

So what's the special occasion?

"Look, you go out on a call, and you never know what you're going to find," says 25-year veteran Curt "Swoop" Nielsen. "So you live large, and you eat large. You want every meal to be really great, because any meal could be your last."

And so it goes in thousands of firehouses all across the country, where firefighters generally work a 24-hour shift—a "watch"—from 8:00 in the morning one day until 8:00 the next morning. Three crews—A, B, and C watches—rotate in sequence with two days off between shifts.

Some days are slow, some insane. Some houses are sleepy, some intense. But there is one common denominator: During those 24 hours of working, waiting, sleeping, anxiety, boredom, laughter, and tragedy, there's always lunch, and there's always dinner.

Visitors are often surprised to learn that most fire departments have no official connection to the food firefighters cook and eat. There are no commissary kitchens, no professional cooks, no department policies dictating who cooks what and when. And perhaps most surprising of all, there is no budget for food. The firefighters pay for it out of their own pockets.

"It's just like anybody going to work and bringing a bag lunch or dinner," says fireboat pilot Bob Costa. "Only where we work, there's a kitchen. Well, officially speaking, there's a stove. Legally, that's the department's end of the bargain. The rest of the kitchen—and the food that goes in and comes out—that's completely up to us."

It's amazing to see what happens in a firehouse when a hot meal's on the table and a run comes in. Forks are dropped in mid-bite, chairs are pushed back, and within seconds, the room is empty. It's been estimated that upwards of half of all firehouse meals are interrupted by a call.

Most houses draw up a chart that assigns one person per watch the task of making both lunch and dinner for the crew on a two- to three-week rotation. That means planning menus, shopping, and cooking. Breakfast is strictly on-your-own and usually relies heavily on leftovers from the night before. Throughout the day, whoever has time on their hands helps with the cooking, and after meals, everyone but the cook does the dishes. At the end of the watch, the crew divides the grocery bill equally. Ten bucks usually covers lunch and dinner.

It's about that simple, and it always has been. If you had a family of 14, you'd probably organize things in much the same way. And that's what makes firehouse food so intensely personal and so emotionally invested.

"What we do is nothing like institutional cooking," says Trace McCulloch, a firefighter who used to work as a cook in several San Francisco restaurants. "It's good home cooking, made with a lot of care, scaled up to feed a bunch of people."

Of course, in San Francisco, "home cooking" has its own special meaning. After all, this is a famous food town. Between the star chefs, the high-profile restaurants, the specialty food shops, the year-round abundance of fresh ingredients, and the ethnically distinct neighborhoods—Hispanic, Asian, African American, Italian, Irish, Eastern European—cooking and eating around here can be pretty exciting. And naturally, so is what goes on in the kitchens of San Francisco's culturally diverse firehouses.

"Look, you go out on a call, and you never know what you're going to find. So you live large, and you eat large. You want every meal to be really great, because any meal could be your last."

Walk into any of the city's 42 fire stations, past the pristine engines and trucks, past the firefighters and officers filling out paperwork, answering the phones, working on equipment, studying for promotional exams, reading, working out, or simply hanging out. And as you reach the back of the house, the smells begin to surprise you.

There, in the open kitchen, amid the joking and ribbing and clanging of pots, you're likely to find someone roasting whole heads of garlic; stirring tamarind paste into a pungent peanut sauce; slathering a whole side of salmon—a fresh chinook they caught the day before just outside the Golden Gate—with olive oil, lemon, and mustard; or pouring a steaming panful of polenta onto the counter to cool. Really.

It's not unusual to see a fire engine double-parked outside the Liguria Bakery in North Beach, where, firefighters will tell you, you'll find the best focaccia in the city. There are seafood wholesalers on the wharf, produce vendors in Chinatown, and meat markets in the Mission District that save the good stuff for their fire department regulars.

Sit down to dinner at a San Francisco firehouse table on a summer night, and you're likely to be treated to grilled pork tenderloin served with spicy green beans with bacon.

Firefighters don't just "borrow the engine" to go shopping out of convenience (though the ability to double-park does come in handy in San Francisco). They have to take "the rig" wherever they go in case they get a call. In fact, when it's one person's turn to shop, the entire crew assigned to that person's rig has to go along for the ride, so they're all together if a call comes in.

Grocery shopping for the firehouse is a bit like a treasure hunt. The challenge: Stay within a one-mile radius of the station and get the best stuff at the best price in the shortest time possible. The secret: From North Beach and Chinatown to the Mission, neighborhood merchants take special care of their SFFD customers, saving the nicest slice, the freshest noodles, the choicest produce, and the best deals for their friends in blue.

In the spring it might be prosciutto-wrapped asparagus, followed by cioppino, the famous San Francisco seafood stew, with chunks of Dungeness crab in the shell; or maybe Thai coconut chicken sprinkled with strips of opal basil, served over jasmine rice. On a foggy fall or winter evening, you might find a soulful skillet paella topped with steamed clams or crisp-skinned rosemary-garlic roast chicken and red potatoes roasted with fresh mint. And anytime of year, you'd want to be sure to save some room for dessert, which runs the gamut from homemade cakes, pies, and cookies to tiramisù.

Every San Francisco firehouse has at least one treasured recipe for Caesar salad (bottled Caesar dressing is unheard of) and at least one unique food tradition. Out at Station 12, near Golden Gate Park, the dinner table is set with a tablecloth and candles, 365 days a year. At Station 29 on Potrero Hill, the crew chipped in to have their old oven door enameled in fire-engine red with gleaming brass trim, by the same body shop that does the department's trucks. The fireboat house, Station 35, perched on Pier 22½ along the Embarcadero, is famous among firefighters for its succulent Chicken in a Barrel, slow-cooked in a custom-made smoker fashioned from an oil drum.

"What we do is nothing like institutional cooking. It's good home cooking, made with a lot of care, scaled up to feed a bunch of people."

Firefighters may not always be able to tell you where these traditions come from, but they honor them religiously and with unabashed pride.

And why not? Food brings people together. And great food, served with pride, holds them together. Firefighter Mike Guajardo sums it up this way: "These are the folks you live, joke, and work with under all kinds of conditions, and for good or bad, cooking for them is a way to show them what you think of them. Sometimes the firehouse is a hectic place. Other times the downtime feels like forever, and the meals are what we have to look forward to. So I say, make them worthwhile each time. Everyone worth hanging out with will always be in the kitchen helping. It's a bonding experience, and at the end of dinner, the compliments let you know no one would mind if you cooked the next watch, too."

The recipes in this book come from people like Mike, Chase, Bob, Trace, and Curt. More often than not, they were slipped to us in secret, faxed from home, recounted in confidence out by the back door of the station. Firefighters aren't big on basking in the limelight. Their pride in their work—and in their cooking—is invariably tempered with humility. Praise is always deflected, credit always shared. As Mike says, "It's a brotherhood thing."

Every dinner is a special occasion at Station 12 near Golden Gate Park, where the table is set with candles and a tablecloth 365 days a year.

Sheila Hunter was a member of the first SFFD Academy class to admit women in 1987. Today, 13% of the force's 1,850 firefighters are women.

A firehouse dinner is often followed by dice games, like 21 and Liar's Dice. They're raucous and fun, but they also serve a purpose—like deciding whether the cost of the meal will be rounded up or down to the nearest dollar or determining who gets to scrub pots and pans.

Early each morning before heading to his job at a local pizza parlor, James, the unofficial "mascot" of Station 16, shows up to raise the flag on the rooftop, polish the vehicles, and do odd jobs around the house. At sunset, he's back to lower the flag. He's even been given his own SFFD uniform.

These are generous, honest, forgiving dishes—easy to prepare, easy to understand, and really easy to enjoy. But what makes them so special is that they've all passed the same test. They've all made people feel happy and helped them connect. This is the food that turns a firehouse into a family.

Somewhere in every firehouse in America, you'll find a copy of "A Fireman's Prayer," a poem written years ago by a now-forgotten author. Like a favorite firehouse recipe, it's been adapted, recopied, and revised over the years. But its simple spirit of generosity remains unchanged. The last verse reads,

And if, according to your will,
I have to lose my life,
Bless with your protecting hand
My loving family from strife.

That's the real inspiration behind firehouse food. It's the food of loving families.

We thank the firefighters of San Francisco for that inspiration, and we hope their food helps bring your friends and family together, too.

About These Recipes

From the moment we began researching this book and visiting San Francisco fire-houses, we knew we had found a very special story to tell. Right from the start, the city's firefighters didn't just want to hand over their recipes. They wanted to talk about them—to tell us where they came from, what makes them so good, and how to make them turn out just right.

In testing and standardizing them for home cooks, we made every effort to preserve the spirit, the intent, and, most importantly, the flavor of the original recipes. What you'll find in this book are great-tasting dishes that are, for the most part, easy and inexpensive to produce. This is unpretentious, satisfying food that's particularly well suited to families and groups. To that end, all of the recipes were written to serve at least six people.

A few notes on ingredients: All recipes that call for broth were tested with canned, low-sodium chicken or beef broth. When recipes call for wine, broth can always be substituted. Rice and pasta, when suggested as an accompaniment, are always included in their raw quantities in the ingredient list, so you'll know how much to start with. Large eggs were used in testing. We recommend using either sea salt or kosher salt, both of which have a cleaner flavor than table salt. For soy sauce, look for "naturally brewed" on the label.

The recipes of San Francisco's firefighters have a life of their own, passing from hand to hand and station to station, constantly changing and evolving as new cooks come along. That never-ending exchange of flavors and ideas is a tradition as old as the department itself—and one we are deeply honored to be a part of.

SALADS & SOUPS

TOMATO MOZZARELLA SALAD

ALISON YEE, ENGINE 12

Alison worked as a caterer in her native England and in Australia before moving to San Francisco and finding her dream career as a firefighter. "It's a wonderfully fulfilling job," she says, "and one of the nicest parts is I didn't have to give up cooking!" She likes to serve this simple salad in the summer when tomatoes are at their best. If you can't find bite-sized fresh mozzarella balls, use larger ones and cut them into ½-inch cubes.

Cut the tomatoes into wedges and put them in a large salad bowl. Add the arugula, mozzarella, and basil. Drizzle the oil and vinegar over the salad and toss to combine. Season to taste with salt and pepper and serve immediately.

Serves 6

1 pound small cluster tomatoes

8 ounces arugula, stems removed

8 ounces bite-sized fresh mozzarella balls *(bocconcini)*

1 cup fresh basil leaves, cut into thin strips

¼ cup extra-virgin olive oil

2 tablespoons balsamic vinegar

Salt and freshly ground black pepper

SLUG SALAD

The casual visitor to a San Francisco firehouse might be alarmed to hear whoever's cooking say, "We're having slug tonight." But any San Francisco firefighter would understand. This bright, tangy salad could even be called the signature dish of the department. No one seems to agree on where it came from, but everyone will tell you that the "slug" part refers to the texture of the mandarin oranges. In SFFD circles, the Girard's Champagne Dressing is nonnegotiable. And so is the name.

To caramelize the almonds: Melt the butter in a small skillet over medium heat. Add the almonds and sauté until golden, about 2 minutes. Add the brown sugar and stir to combine. Spread the almonds on a baking sheet, separating them. Set aside to cool. When completely cooled, the almonds will have a hard, candied coating.

To assemble the salad: In a large salad bowl, toss the lettuce with the red onion, blue cheese, mandarin oranges, and dressing to taste. Sprinkle the almonds over the salad and serve immediately.

Serves 6

CARAMELIZED ALMONDS

2 teaspoons butter

1/3 cup slivered almonds

2 tablespoons brown sugar

2 heads butter lettuce, washed and torn into bite-sized pieces

1/2 small red onion, thinly sliced

4 ounces blue cheese, crumbled

2 cans (11 ounces each) mandarin oranges, drained

Girard's Champagne Dressing

CHINESE CHICKEN SALAD

TERRY WOO, AIRPORT RESCUE 1

The dressing for this salad is known throughout the department as T. Woo's Green Goddess. Terry's poaching method is a foolproof way to make tender, succulent chicken for salads and sandwiches.

To poach the chicken breasts: Put the breasts in a medium saucepan with the soy sauce and just enough water to cover the chicken. Bring to a boil, cover, and remove from the heat. Let stand, covered, for 30 minutes. Remove the chicken breasts from the poaching liquid and reserve the liquid for another use. Let the chicken cool, then tear the meat into bite-sized pieces.

To make the dressing: Combine the mayonnaise, sugar, vinegar, sesame oil, soy sauce, cayenne, garlic, ginger, and cilantro in a blender or food processor and purée until smooth. Refrigerate until ready to use.

To assemble the salad: In a large salad bowl, toss the chicken with the lettuce, carrots, noodles, and dressing. Top each serving with some of the caramelized almonds and sesame seeds.

Serves 6 as a first course or 4 as a main course

4 boneless, skinless chicken breast halves (about 1½ pound total)

3 tablespoons soy sauce

DRESSING

1 cup mayonnaise

1 tablespoon sugar

3 tablespoons rice wine vinegar

2 tablespoons Asian sesame oil

2 tablespoons soy sauce

Pinch of cayenne pepper

3 cloves garlic, chopped

1 piece fresh ginger, about 1 inch long, peeled and minced

1 bunch cilantro, leaves only (about 1 cup)

1 head iceberg lettuce, chopped

3 medium carrots, peeled and grated

1½ cups crispy chow mein noodles

⅓ cup Caramelized Almonds (page 34) or slivered almonds, toasted (see page 163)

1 tablespoon sesame seeds, toasted (see page 173)

"SOMETHING DIFFERENT" SALAD STEVE MILLER, ENGINE 34

This is a summertime favorite at Station 34, way out on the western edge of the city, where, on those rare afternoons when the fog lifts, you can look out at the Pacific while you're barbecuing on the patio. After years of firehouse salad making, Steve made this discovery: Typical salad ingredients take on a lot more flavor when you layer them in a dish and give them a good soak in just about any kind of vinaigrette, then serve them over greens. "People really go for it," he says. "Maybe because they like putting their own salad together just the way they want it. Or maybe just because it's something different."

Toss the avocado slices in the lemon juice to coat. Layer the sliced avocado in a 9-by-13-inch glass baking dish. Layer the tomato slices over the avocado. Top with the red onion. Sprinkle the basil and feta over the top.

To make the vinaigrette: Put the vinegar in a small bowl and drizzle in the olive oil while whisking. Stir in the shallot and add salt and pepper to taste. Pour the vinaigrette over the layered salad mixture; cover and refrigerate for 2 to 3 hours.

To serve, divide the greens evenly among 6 plates and let each person top his or her greens with some of the layered salad and the vinaigrette from the baking dish.

Serves 6

3 avocados, pitted, peeled, and cut crosswise into 1/4-inch slices

2 tablespoons freshly squeezed lemon juice

3 medium tomatoes, cut crosswise into 1/4-inch-thick slices

1/2 small red onion, thinly sliced

1/2 cup fresh basil leaves, cut into thin strips

4 ounces feta cheese, crumbled

12 ounces mixed salad greens, washed and chilled

STEVE'S BALSAMIC VINAIGRETTE

1/4 cup balsamic vinegar

3/4 cup extra-virgin olive oil

1 large shallot, minced

Salt and freshly ground black pepper

THE HOUSE SALAD

Sit down to a firehouse dinner at 7:00, and chances are you'll still be at the table at 9:00. "Dinner's one of the high points of our job," says firefighter Steve Feiner, "and we're here all night, so why not make it last?" That could explain why the meal almost always starts with a relaxed salad course. Usually it takes the form of an enormous bowl heaped with just-washed greens tossed in a homemade dressing, with all kinds of tasty extras thrown in for flavor and texture—golden cherry tomatoes, toasted nuts, goat cheese, olives, avocados. "Fresh" is the operative word. After all, this is California.

HONEY-DILL VINAIGRETTE

GEORGE JOSEPH PETTY III, ENGINE 23

Firehouse cooks often make salad dressing in the blender—an easy way to emulsify all the ingredients. This versatile dressing goes well with salads that include nuts, pumpkin seeds (page 43), and dried fruit, or try it with ripe tomatoes, green onions, and cucumbers. It will keep for a week or more in an airtight container in the refrigerator.

½ cup balsamic vinegar

¼ cup honey

4 cloves garlic, chopped

1 tablespoon dried dill

1 cup olive oil

Salt and freshly ground black pepper

Put the vinegar, honey, garlic, and dill in the container of a blender or food processor and process until smooth. With the machine running, add the olive oil in a thin, steady stream until it is completely emulsified. Season to taste with salt and pepper.

Makes about 1¾ cups

SALLY'S SALAD DRESSING

SALLY SAXTON, ENGINE 34

Sally likes to serve this all-purpose vinaigrette with a mixture of romaine and baby greens, tossed with cherry tomatoes, toasted almonds, dried cranberries, and a special feta cheese made with tomato and basil. The dressing will keep for a week or more in an airtight container in the refrigerator.

¼ cup red wine vinegar

1 tablespoon Dijon mustard

2 cloves garlic, minced or pressed

Pinch of dried basil

Pinch of dried marjoram

½ cup extra-virgin olive oil

Salt and freshly ground black pepper

In a medium bowl, whisk together the vinegar, mustard, garlic, basil, and marjoram. Slowly add the olive oil in a thin, steady stream, whisking constantly to form an emulsion. Season to taste with salt and pepper.

Makes about 1¾ cups

BUTTERMILK RANCH DRESSING

SFFD CLASSIC

Use this all-American classic on hearty greens, like red romaine or iceberg lettuce. It's good with just about any kind of chicken salad, too. Add a little extra sour cream and you can use it as a dip for fresh vegetables. It will keep for up to 5 days in an airtight container in the refrigerator.

$1/2$ cup buttermilk

$1/2$ cup sour cream

1 cup mayonnaise

$1/4$ cup olive oil

$1/4$ cup cider vinegar

1 clove garlic, chopped

1 teaspoon dry mustard

1 teaspoon dried dill

1 teaspoon dried thyme

$1/2$ teaspoon salt

$1/2$ teaspoon freshly ground black pepper

Dash of Tabasco sauce

$1/4$ cup chopped parsley

Put the buttermilk, sour cream, mayonnaise, oil, vinegar, garlic, dry mustard, dill, thyme, salt, pepper, and Tabasco in the container of a blender or food processor and process until smooth. Stir in the chopped parsley.

Makes about 2 3/4 cups

CALAMARI SALAD

TONY SERPA, TRUCK 6

Fresh calamari are definitely the way to go when they're in season. The flavor and texture are well worth the work it takes to clean them. This recipe calls for draining off the excess marinade, but you might prefer to leave it in and serve this salad in a deep plate with a piece of sourdough bread to soak up all the juices.

To clean and prepare the calamari: Pull the tentacles away from the body of each squid. Cut the tentacles just below the eyes and discard the eyes, the head, and the small rib piece from the center of the tentacles. Extract and discard the quill and innards from the body piece. Peel away the thin membrane from the body under cold running water; discard the membrane. Rinse and drain the body and tentacle pieces. Cut the bodies into 1/2-inch rings and the larger tentacle pieces in half.

Prepare an ice bath by filling a large bowl with water and ice. Bring a large pot of water to a boil. Add some salt and the cleaned calamari. Cook for 3 minutes and remove with a slotted spoon to the ice water bath; let cool for 5 minutes before draining.

In a large bowl, mix the calamari with the bell peppers, garlic, parsley, capers, onion, oil, and vinegar. Season to taste with salt and pepper. Marinate in the refrigerator for 3 to 4 hours. Just before serving, drain off the excess liquid.

Serves 6

3 pounds fresh calamari

1 red bell pepper, stemmed, seeded, and cut into 1/4-inch slices

1 yellow bell pepper, stemmed, seeded, and cut into 1/4-inch slices

1 green bell pepper, stemmed, seeded, and cut into 1/4-inch slices

4 cloves garlic, finely chopped

1/2 bunch Italian parsley, chopped

1/4 cup capers

1 medium red onion, halved and thinly sliced

1 cup extra-virgin olive oil

1/2 cup red wine vinegar

Sea salt and freshly ground black pepper

MEXICAN CHICKEN SALAD

MARTY VERHAEG, ENGINE 13

Marty likes to make this salad for lunch because it's a "whole meal-in-one kind of thing." If you're feeling ambitious, serve it tostada-style over crisp, freshly fried corn tortillas. Or just set out a big bowl of tortilla chips to eat with the salad, and you'll get roughly the same effect.

Adjust the oven rack to the center position and preheat the oven to 375°F.

With a meat pounder or a heavy skillet, lightly pound each chicken breast between sheets of waxed paper or plastic wrap to a thickness of about 1/4 inch.

Combine the flour, cumin, chili powder, and oregano in a small bowl, then spread this mixture on a large plate. Spread the bread crumbs on a second large plate. Pour the milk into a wide, shallow bowl. Pour the eggs into another wide, shallow bowl. Dip one chicken breast into the milk and dredge it in the flour mixture, shaking off any excess. Dip the floured chicken breast in the egg and then the bread crumbs, coating it thoroughly on both sides. Repeat with the remaining chicken breasts.

Heat the oil in a large nonstick skillet over medium heat. Cook the chicken breasts until lightly brown on both sides, about 2 minutes per side. Transfer the breasts to a baking dish and finish cooking in the oven for 15 minutes. Then transfer the chicken to a cutting board and let cool. Cut the chicken on the diagonal into 3/8-inch slices.

To assemble the salad: toss the lettuce with the tomatoes, olives, onion, avocado, and dressing. Season to taste with salt and pepper. Top with the grated cheese and chicken.

Serves 6

4 boneless, skinless chicken breast halves (about 2 pounds total)

1/2 cup all-purpose flour

1 teaspoon ground cumin

1 teaspoon chili powder

1 teaspoon dried oregano

1 cup bread crumbs

1/2 cup milk

2 eggs, beaten

1/4 cup olive oil

2 heads romaine lettuce, outer leaves removed, torn into bite-sized pieces

1 cup cherry tomatoes, halved

1/4 cup sliced black olives

1 small red onion, thinly sliced

1 avocado, pitted, peeled, and sliced crosswise

1 cup Buttermilk Ranch Dressing (page 39)

Salt and freshly ground black pepper

1/2 cup grated sharp Cheddar cheese

"MEXICAN RESTAURANT" SALAD CHASE WILSON, ENGINE 32

Chase and her friends love the romaine salad with a creamy cilantro dressing served at a popular San Francisco Mexican restaurant. So they got together and figured out how to make it at home. *Queso fresco,* a crumbly white Mexican cheese, is sold in Mexican markets and many supermarkets. If you can't find it, substitute a mild feta.

To make the dressing: Put the lime juice, olive oil, mayonnaise, sour cream, cilantro, jalapeño, garlic, cumin, chili powder, and Parmesan in the container of a blender or food processor; process until smooth. Refrigerate until ready to use.

To toast the pumpkin seeds: Heat the olive oil in a small skillet and add the pumpkin seeds. Toss continuously until the seeds are lightly toasted, about 3 minutes. Season to taste with salt and let cool.

To assemble the salad: Combine the lettuce, onion, avocado, tortilla chips, and dressing in a large salad bowl. Season to taste with salt and pepper. Sprinkle the *queso fresco* and toasted pumpkin seeds over the salad.

Serves 6

CILANTRO–SOUR CREAM DRESSING

2 tablespoons freshly squeezed lime juice

1/2 cup olive oil

2 tablespoons mayonnaise

2 tablespoons sour cream

1/2 cup stemmed, coarsely chopped cilantro (about 1/2 bunch)

1 green jalapeño chile, stemmed, seeded, and deribbed

2 cloves garlic, chopped

1/4 teaspoon ground cumin

1/4 teaspoon chili powder

2 tablespoons grated Parmesan cheese

1 teaspoon olive oil

1/4 cup pumpkin seeds

Salt

2 heads romaine lettuce, outer leaves removed, torn into bite-sized pieces

1 small red onion, thinly sliced

1 avocado, pitted, peeled, and cubed

1 1/2 cups yellow corn tortilla chips, lightly crushed

Freshly ground black pepper

4 ounces *queso fresco,* crumbled

IN THIS TOWN, CAESAR RULES

It seems there's hardly a restaurant in San Francisco that doesn't serve a Caesar salad, and maybe that's why the same can be said of the city's firehouses. But as firefighter Mike Beere says, "I've never had a restaurant Caesar as good as the ones we make."

Every house has at least one "official" Caesar recipe and plenty of opinions on how to put the salad together. At Station 12, John Hicks's 'Chovie Blue calls for blue cheese in place of the traditional Parmesan, and John Clifford tosses the romaine leaves in fresh lemon juice before adding the dressing for an extra hit of citrus flavor. Cliff Merrill at 28 gets the same effect by rubbing the plates with the cut surface of a lemon. At Station 16, Mike Guajardo gives his C-Watch Caesar an extra kick by adding a little balsamic vinegar and oregano. Sal Taormina at 31 replaces all but a tablespoon of the oil with low-fat yogurt to create his Healthy Caesar.

What follows is a composite of several recipes made throughout the department. It's a fine base for starting a few "house Caesar" traditions of your own.

FIREHOUSE CAESAR SALAD SFFD CLASSIC

If you're concerned about using raw eggs, you can substitute $^1/_3$ cup mayonnaise for the eggs in this dressing. If you're a fan of garlic and anchovies (like most San Francisco firefighters), add more of them to taste.

Adjust the oven rack to the center position and preheat the oven to 350°F.

To make the croutons: Put the garlic and olive oil in the container of a blender or a food processor fitted with the metal blade. Pulse until the garlic is puréed. Pour into a large bowl and toss with the bread cubes, coating them evenly. Season to taste with salt and pepper. Spread the bread cubes in a single layer on a baking sheet and bake, stirring occasionally, until light golden brown, about 12 minutes. Let cool to room temperature.

To make the dressing: Put the eggs, lemon juice, mustard, vinegar, Worcestershire sauce, garlic, anchovies, and Parmesan in the container of a blender or food processor and purée. With the motor running, add the oil in a very thin, steady stream, to form a smooth emulsion. Season to taste with salt and pepper. (You should have 2 cups.)

To assemble the salad: Put the lettuce and croutons in a large salad bowl. Gradually add the dressing (you will not need all of it) and toss to combine until the leaves are coated. Toss in most of the Parmesan. Taste and add salt and pepper if needed. Sprinkle the remaining Parmesan over the salad.

Serves 6 to 8

CROUTONS

4 cloves garlic, chopped

$^1/_4$ cup olive oil

1 baguette or loaf of French bread, cut into 1-inch cubes (to make about 4 cups)

Salt and freshly ground black pepper

DRESSING

2 eggs

2 tablespoons freshly squeezed lemon juice

2 tablespoons Dijon mustard

1 tablespoon red wine vinegar

1 tablespoon Worcestershire sauce

2 to 3 cloves garlic, chopped

6 anchovy fillets

$^1/_4$ cup grated Parmesan cheese

1 cup extra-virgin olive oil

Salt and freshly ground black pepper

3 heads romaine lettuce, outer leaves removed, cut or torn into bite-sized pieces

$^1/_2$ cup grated Parmesan cheese

TIM'S LOUIS SALAD

LT. TIM CALLEN, TRUCK 16

Firefighting and cooking are long-standing traditions in the Callen family. Tim's grandfather John Bogue Sr. served in the department for 48 years, and his culinary talents were immortalized in several recipes in the 1965 *San Francisco Firehouse Favorites* cookbook. Tim works at Station 16 on Greenwich Street in the Marina, just a few minutes from the wharf, and when he's cooking, he'll often start the day with a trip to La Rocca Seafood for a little shrimp or fresh-cracked Dungeness crab—and a lot of wisecracking. His classic Louis Salad can be made with shrimp, crab, or a combination of the two.

Put 6 salad plates in the freezer to chill.

To make the dressing: Whisk together the mayonnaise, ketchup, Worcestershire sauce, Tabasco sauce, mustard, vinegar, lemon juice, pepper, garlic powder, and cayenne. Cover and refrigerate until ready to use.

To cook the beets: Put the beets in a small saucepan with enough water to cover them. Bring to a boil and cook until tender, about 30 minutes. Drain in a colander and let cool. Peel the beets with your fingers under cold running water. Cut into 1/4-inch-thick slices and set aside.

To cook the asparagus: Prepare an ice bath by filling a large bowl with water and ice. Bring a large pot of lightly salted water to a boil. Add the asparagus and cook until crisp-tender, about 2 minutes. Using a slotted spoon, transfer the asparagus to the ice bath. When the asparagus spears have cooled, drain them in a colander, then lay them on paper towels to absorb any excess moisture. Set aside until ready to use.

Serves 6

LOUIS DRESSING

1/2 cup mayonnaise

1/3 cup ketchup

1 tablespoon Worcestershire sauce

1 teaspoon Tabasco sauce

1 tablespoon Dijon mustard

1 teaspoon balsamic vinegar

Juice of 1 lemon

1/2 teaspoon freshly ground black pepper

1/4 teaspoon garlic powder

Pinch of cayenne pepper

2 medium beets

1 pound asparagus, ends trimmed

2 heads butter lettuce

2 cups cherry tomatoes, halved

To assemble the salad: Tear the lettuce into bite-sized pieces. In a large salad bowl, toss the lettuce with the tomatoes, green onions, and half of the dressing. Divide the salad among the 6 chilled plates and arrange the beets, asparagus, shrimp, avocado, and eggs on top of each serving. Drizzle some of the remaining dressing over each salad. Garnish with the lemon wedges.

3 green onions, white and pale green parts only, chopped

2 pounds cooked bay shrimp or crabmeat

2 avocados, pitted, peeled, and sliced

3 hard-boiled eggs, peeled, and sliced

1 lemon, cut into 6 wedges, for garnish

ROASTED BEET SALAD with RASPBERRY BALSAMIC VINAIGRETTE

TRACE McCULLOCH, ENGINE 21

Roasted beets sound fancy, but they're easy to make and have a lot more flavor than boiled or canned beets. Trace's Raspberry Balsamic Vinaigrette brings out their sweetness and ties everything together.

To roast the beets: Adjust the oven rack to the center position and preheat the oven to 400°F. Rub the beets with the olive oil and wrap them together in a large piece of aluminum foil. Put the beets in a small roasting pan or baking dish and roast them for 50 minutes to an hour, until they are tender when a knife is inserted in the center. Remove the foil packet from the pan and let the beets cool on the foil before unwrapping. Using your fingers, peel the beets over the foil. The skins should slip off easily; if not, use a paring knife. Cut the beets into $1/4$-inch matchstick slices and reserve.

To make the vinaigrette: Put the olive oil, balsamic vinegar, red wine vinegar, onion, jam, mustard, and sugar in the container of a blender or food processor. Process until well blended and emulsified. (You should have 1 cup.) Season to taste with salt and pepper.

To assemble the salad: In a large salad bowl, toss the greens, beets, and walnuts with half of the dressing. Season to taste with pepper. Top each serving with some of the cheese. Pass the remaining dressing at the table.

Serves 6

6 medium beets (red, gold, or a
   combination; about 1$1/2$ pounds
   total), stemmed

1 tablespoon olive oil

RASPBERRY BALSAMIC VINAIGRETTE

$3/4$ cup olive oil

3 tablespoons balsamic vinegar

1 tablespoon red wine vinegar

3 tablespoons minced red onion

2 tablespoons raspberry jam

2 tablespoons Dijon mustard

$1/2$ teaspoon sugar

Salt and freshly ground black pepper

8 ounces "spring mix" salad greens

1 cup walnuts, toasted (see page 163)

Freshly ground black pepper

6 ounces Gorgonzola cheese, crumbled

MIXED GREENS with PEARS and DRIED CRANBERRIES

TRACE McCULLOCH, ENGINE 21

You'll find a variation of this salad with a sweet vinaigrette, fruit, and nuts at firehouses all over San Francisco. Trace refers to his version by the unassuming name Fruit Salad. That's firefighter modesty for you. It's actually a sophisticated sweet-tangy-crunchy combination that tastes like something Trace might have served back in the days when he was a professional chef. He suggests using tart green apples if you can't find good pears.

To make the dressing: In a small bowl, whisk together the vinegar, honey, mustard, and sugar. Slowly drizzle in the olive oil, whisking continuously to form a smooth emulsion. Season to taste with salt and pepper.

To assemble the salad: In a large salad bowl, toss the greens, pear slices, red onion, cranberries, and goat cheese with the dressing. Taste the salad and season again with salt and pepper, if needed; garnish with the almonds.

Serves 6

DRESSING

¹/₄ cup cider vinegar

2 teaspoons honey

2 teaspoons Dijon mustard

¹/₂ teaspoon sugar

³/₄ cup olive oil

Salt and freshly ground black pepper

1 pound mixed salad greens (such as red leaf lettuce, butter lettuce, baby spinach, or arugula)

2 medium Bosc or Anjou pears, cored, quartered, and thinly sliced crosswise

1 small red onion, thinly sliced

¹/₂ cup dried cranberries

4 ounces goat cheese, crumbled

Salt and freshly ground black pepper

¹/₃ cup sliced almonds, toasted (see page 163)

CALDO DE RES

CAPT. RICH JOHNSON, ENGINE 26

In Mexico, a *caldo* is a meaty one-bowl meal that falls somewhere on the spectrum between a soup and a stew. The reason this one tastes so authentic is its source: Rich persuaded the owner of a now-closed San Francisco *taquería* to share his house recipe. If you prefer a hearty chicken soup, substitute chicken broth and boneless, skinless chicken thighs (and change the name to Caldo de Pollo).

Heat the oil in a large, heavy pot over medium-high heat; add the meat and brown on all sides, about 5 minutes. Add the onion and garlic and cook for 3 minutes. Add the tomatoes, broth, bay leaf, and oregano. Bring to a boil and reduce the heat to a simmer. Cook for 1½ hours, partially covered.

Stir in the potatoes, carrot, and corn; continue to cook for 30 minutes. Add the zucchini, cabbage, and cilantro; cook for 15 minutes. Discard the bay leaf and season to taste with salt and pepper. Ladle the soup into warm bowls and pass the diced onion, cilantro, lime wedges, and tortillas at the table.

Hill Houses: San Francisco is famous for its hills, and several of its firehouses are perched on top of them. The "hill house" tradition dates back to the days of horse-drawn hook-and-ladders, when racing downhill to a fire rather than uphill made all the difference in saving lives and property.

Serves 6

2 tablespoons vegetable oil

2½ pounds beef chuck steak, cut into ½-inch cubes

1 medium white onion, diced

3 cloves garlic, chopped

1 can (14½ ounces) diced tomatoes

6 cups beef broth

1 bay leaf

1 tablespoon dried Mexican oregano

1 pound red potatoes, diced

1 carrot, peeled and diced

2 ears corn, shucked and cut into 1-inch-thick rounds

1 zucchini, cut into thick matchsticks, 1 inch long

½ head green cabbage, cored, thinly sliced

¼ cup chopped cilantro

Salt and freshly ground black pepper

ACCOMPANIMENTS

½ medium white onion, finely diced

Cilantro sprigs

1 lime, cut into 6 wedges

12 fresh tortillas, warmed (see page 73)

BEEF BARLEY SOUP

LT. DENISE NEWMAN, ENGINE 32

On a chilly day, Denise likes to get this soul-warming soup going at the beginning of the watch and serve it a few hours later as a hearty lunch with crusty sourdough bread, a green salad, and whatever fresh fruit is in season.

In a large, heavy-bottomed soup pot or Dutch oven, heat the oil and brown the cubes of beef in small batches, seasoning each batch with salt and pepper. Use a slotted spoon to transfer the browned beef to a bowl, leaving as much fat in the pot as possible.

Once all the meat has been browned and removed, add the onion, celery, carrot, and $1/4$ cup parsley to the pot; cover and cook over medium heat, stirring occasionally, for about 5 minutes, until the vegetables are soft.

Return the beef to the pot along with any juices that have collected in the bowl. Add the broth, barley, tomatoes (with their liquid), Worcestershire sauce, bay leaves, and thyme. Bring the soup to a boil, then lower the heat and simmer for $1^{1}/_{2}$ hours, stirring occasionally and adding water if the soup becomes too thick.

Skim any fat that has risen to the surface of the soup, discard the bay leaves, and season with salt and pepper to taste. Ladle into bowls and garnish with the remaining parsley.

Serves 6

2 tablespoons olive or vegetable oil

1 pound London broil or beef chuck roast, cut into $1/2$-inch cubes

Salt and freshly ground black pepper

1 small onion, cut into $1/4$-inch dice

3 stalks celery, cut into $1/4$-inch dice

1 large carrot, peeled and cut into $1/4$-inch dice

$1/4$ cup chopped parsley, plus 1 tablespoon for garnish

6 cups beef broth

1 cup pearl barley

1 can (14$1/2$ ounces) diced tomatoes

1 tablespoon Worcestershire sauce

3 bay leaves

$1/2$ teaspoon dried thyme

TORTILLA SOUP

MARTY VERHAEG, ENGINE 13

This Mexican chicken-and-tomato soup makes a satisfying hot lunch or light supper. Marty says this recipe has been floating around the department for about as long as he can remember. Everyone adds their own twists and touches, and as far as Marty knows, no one has ever written it down—until now.

Put the chicken in a large, heavy stockpot with the broth. Bring to a boil, then reduce to a simmer and cook until the chicken is tender and pulls away from the bone easily, about 45 minutes. Transfer the chicken pieces to a plate and let cool. Remove the meat from the bones and tear or cut into bite-sized pieces. Set aside until ready to use. Pour the broth through a fine-mesh strainer into a bowl and skim as much fat as possible from the surface.

In the now-empty stockpot, heat 2 tablespoons of the vegetable oil over medium heat and sauté the diced onion until soft, about 3 minutes. Stir in the chiles and cumin and cook for 5 minutes. Add the stewed tomatoes, tomato sauce, strained chicken broth, and rice. Bring to a boil, then reduce to a simmer and cook for 20 minutes.

While the soup is cooking, heat the remaining 1/2 cup vegetable oil in a skillet over medium-high heat. Test the oil by dropping a tortilla strip into it. If it sizzles, the oil is ready. Fry the tortilla strips in small batches until golden brown, removing them with a slotted spoon to a paper towel. Set aside until ready to serve.

Add the chicken and corn kernels to the soup. Simmer for 20 minutes more. Stir in the cilantro and season to taste with salt and pepper. Ladle into warm bowls and top with the tortilla strips, diced avocado, and grated cheese. Serve each bowl with a lime wedge on the side.

Serves 6

1 frying chicken (about 5 pounds), cut up and skin removed

8 cups chicken broth

1/2 cup, plus 2 tablespoons vegetable oil

1 medium white onion, diced

2 fresh pasilla chiles, roasted (see page 141), stemmed, seeded, and diced or 1 can (7 ounces) diced roasted green chiles

1 teaspoon ground cumin

1 can (14 1/2 ounces) Mexican-style stewed tomatoes

1 can (15 ounces) tomato sauce

1/4 cup short-grain rice, preferably Arborio

3 corn tortillas, halved and cut crosswise into 1/4-inch strips

1 cup fresh or frozen corn kernels

1/2 cup chopped cilantro

Salt and freshly ground black pepper

ACCOMPANIMENTS

1 avocado, pitted, peeled, and diced

1/2 cup grated Monterey Jack cheese or 1 cup sour cream

1 lime, cut into 6 wedges

DUCK WONTON SOUP

JOHN CHUNG, ENGINE 17

John likes to make wontons from scratch at the firehouse, and with a little help from firefighters Norm Kwan and Ramon Chea, the work goes quickly. This recipe is a combination of what each of them learned from their mothers. Folding wontons is surprisingly easy. If you can't master the classic fold, just gather the wrapper around the filling and pinch it to form a bundle. Look for roast duck in Chinese delis. It's sold whole or hacked into small pieces to order—bones and all—which is how John buys it for soup. If it's not available where you live, substitute roast chicken.

To make the wonton filling: In a large bowl, mix the pork, green onions, water chestnuts, snow peas, ginger, Worcestershire sauce, soy sauce, sesame oil, and egg until well combined.

To make the wontons: Lay a wonton wrapper on the work surface with a corner facing you. Lightly brush the top 2 edges with a little of the diluted beaten egg. Place a teaspoon of the filling in the center and fold the wonton wrapper over it, forming a triangle. Press the edges together to seal. Brush a little egg on the corners of the folded edge, and bring the 2 corners down, overlapping one over the other and pinching them together to seal. Repeat with the remaining wrappers and filling. (You should have 72 wontons.)

Bring a large pot of water to a boil. Fill a large bowl with cold water and place it nearby. Cook the wontons in the boiling water in batches of 24 for 2½ minutes per batch; remove each batch with a slotted spoon and transfer the wontons to the cold water. Drain and set aside.

continued on page 60

Serves 8

WONTON FILLING

6 ounces ground pork

3 green onions, white and pale green parts only, finely chopped

2 tablespoons finely chopped water chestnuts

1 ounce fresh snow peas, strings removed, finely chopped

2 tablespoons grated fresh ginger

1 tablespoon Worcestershire sauce

2 tablespoons soy sauce

1 tablespoon Asian sesame oil

1 egg lightly beaten

1 pound wonton wrappers

1 egg beaten with 2 tablespoons water

"When I'm cooking, the first decision is not what's on the menu," says John. "It's what music is on the stereo." That's understandable: For the last 20 years, he's been moonlighting as a DJ at a Bay Area radio station where he hosts a popular jazz program.

To make the soup: In a large pot, bring the broth to a boil and whisk in the miso paste, stirring to dissolve. Stir in the wontons, duck pieces, and bok choy. Cook for 3 minutes, stirring occasionally. Ladle the soup into warmed bowls, garnish with the sliced green onions, and serve immediately.

SOUP

12 cups chicken broth

¼ cup miso paste

1 Chinese roast duck, cut into small pieces

1¼ pounds baby bok choy, stemmed, rinsed, and leaves separated

2 green onions, white and pale green parts only, thinly sliced on the diagonal, for garnish

HOME-STYLE JOOK

MICHAEL CARION, ENGINE 14

"You wouldn't believe it, but a cup of rice can feed six people," says Michael. In fact, depending on where you buy your chicken legs, this homey, comforting Chinese soup can be made for around two dollars. Michael's family moved to San Francisco from Hong Kong when he was a year old, and he learned this recipe by osmosis in the family kitchen. "I didn't try it out at the firehouse for a long time," he says. "And when I finally did, everyone was kind of skeptical. But now, they're always asking me to make it." He serves it as a first course, then follows it with a main dish, like his Kung Pao Prawns (page 124), and a stir-fried vegetable.

Wash the rice in several changes of cold water until the water is no longer cloudy. Drain the rice and put it in a large, heavy-bottomed soup pot. Add the water and broth. Bring to a boil and immediately reduce the heat to low. Simmer, uncovered, for 1 hour, stirring occasionally.

In a small skillet, fry the pork over medium heat, breaking it up into very small pieces. Add the pork, chicken, and salt to the soup. Simmer for about 2 hours more, stirring from time to time, until the soup is the consistency of a thin, creamy porridge. As it thickens, you will need to stir the soup more frequently and keep a close eye on it to prevent burning or sticking. Remove the chicken leg from the pot and discard the skin and bones; shred the meat and stir it into the soup.

Combine the cilantro, green onions, and pepper in a small bowl. Ladle the soup into bowls, garnishing each serving with a bit of the cilantro mixture. Pass the ginger and soy sauce at the table to accompany the soup.

Serves 6

1 cup long-grain white rice

4 quarts water

2 cups chicken broth

4 ounces ground pork

1 chicken leg

1 tablespoon salt

2 tablespoons coarsely chopped cilantro

2 green onions, white and pale green parts only, thinly sliced

1/2 teaspoon white pepper

ACCOMPANIMENTS

1 piece fresh ginger, about 1 inch long, peeled and cut into thin slivers

Soy sauce

MAIN DISHES

ORANGE and GINGER GRILLED PORK TENDERLOIN

MIKE GUAJARDO, ENGINE 16

This is one of those simple recipes you can count on as the main event of a special dinner. On the side, try Spicy Green Beans with Bacon (page 155) and Roasted–Garlic & Sour Cream Mashed Potatoes (page 170). Make extra—sliced thin and drizzled with the sauce, the meat is great in sandwiches the next day. This recipe actually works best with an inexpensive sweet orange marmalade rather than the Seville variety.

To make the marinade: Combine the orange juice, vinegar, ginger, and orange zest in a small bowl.

Put the pork tenderloins in a shallow pan and pour the marinade over them. Refrigerate for 4 to 6 hours.

To make the Orange-Ginger Sauce: Melt the marmalade in a small pan. Add the ginger, soy sauce, cider vinegar, and mustard, stirring to combine; keep warm.

Prepare the grill with a medium-hot fire (see page 99). Remove the meat from the marinade and season it with salt and pepper. Grill, turning at least once, until an instant-read thermometer inserted in the center of the meat reads 150°F, 15 to 20 minutes. Brush with some of the Orange-Ginger Sauce during the last 5 minutes of cooking. Allow the meat to rest on a cutting board tented with aluminum foil for a few minutes before slicing. Slice the meat 1/2 inch thick on the diagonal. Pass the remaining sauce at the table.

Serves 6 to 8

MARINADE

1 cup orange juice

1/4 cup cider vinegar

1 tablespoon finely grated fresh ginger

2 tablespoons grated orange zest

3 pork tenderloins (about 3 pounds total)

ORANGE-GINGER SAUCE

1 cup sweet orange marmalade

1 tablespoon finely grated fresh ginger

2 tablespoons light soy sauce

2 tablespoons cider vinegar

1 tablespoon Dijon mustard

Salt and freshly ground black pepper

POT ROAST with RED SAUCE LT. ED DEA, DIVISION OF TRAINING

"When I was working in the field," says Ed (who now trains new recruits at the SFFD Academy), "I built the whole meal around what was on sale." Often that turned out to be a roast, and Ed perfected all kinds of ways to cook them. This tender, juicy one braises slowly in marinara sauce, and you can serve it over pasta or toss the pasta in the sauce and serve it separately. If you have time, make the marinara from scratch; if you don't, a store-bought sauce will give you great results, too. Just be sure to find one that's on sale.

Preheat the oven to 350°F. Trim any excess fat from the roast and rub it with the garlic salt. Coat the roast with the flour. Heat the oil in a large skillet and brown the roast on all sides. Transfer the roast to a 9-by-13-inch roasting pan.

Pour the water into the skillet and cook over medium-high heat for 1 minute, scraping up any browned bits from the bottom. Add the marinara sauce to the skillet, stir to combine, and pour the mixture over the roast. Cover the roasting pan with aluminum foil and cut two 1-inch slits in the foil to allow steam to escape. Put the pan on a baking sheet to catch any drips; bake until the roast is cooked through and very tender when pierced with a fork, about 2 hours and 15 minutes.

When the roast is done, cook the rigatoni according to the package directions.

Transfer the roast to a cutting board. Let rest for 10 minutes, loosely tented with the aluminum foil, before slicing. Meanwhile, transfer the sauce to a saucepan over medium-high heat and cook until reduced and thickened slightly; season to taste with salt, if needed, and pepper.

Serve the sliced pot roast and sauce over the rigatoni.

Serves 6

1 boneless beef chuck roast
  (3 to 4 pounds)

1 tablespoon garlic salt

1/4 cup all-purpose flour

2 tablespoons vegetable oil

3 cups water or beef broth

4 cups Marinara Sauce (page 136,
  prepared without the ground
  turkey)

1 pound dried rigatoni

Salt and freshly ground black pepper

OXTAIL OSSOBUCO

JASON HARRELL, ENGINE 39

Ossobuco is traditionally made with veal shanks, but Jason makes this hearty version with oxtails, which are more intensely flavored and usually a lot more affordable. Like most braised dishes, it's even better the second day. Serve it over buttered egg noodles or Creamy Polenta (page 172).

Preheat the oven to 350°F.

Heat the olive oil over medium heat in a large, heavy-bottomed soup pot or Dutch oven with a tight-fitting lid. Season the oxtails with salt and pepper and lightly brown them in the oil on all sides. Use a slotted spoon to transfer the browned meat to a plate, leaving as much fat in the pot as possible.

Add the onions, garlic, carrots, leek, and celery to the pot and sauté until tender, about 10 minutes. Stir in the parsley, tomatoes, tomato sauce, vinegar, sugar, red pepper flakes, bay leaves, Italian seasoning, onion powder, garlic powder, and oregano. Bring to a simmer and cook for 15 minutes. Add the oxtails, cover the pot, and place it in the oven. Cook until the meat is very tender, about 2 hours. Discard the bay leaves and season to taste with salt and pepper.

Door Slammers: Because firehouse cooking has to be juggled with an unpredictable work schedule, many firefighters rely on the time-honored tradition of "door slammers"—dishes like pot roast that can be thrown in the oven and ignored, if need be, till dinnertime.

Serves 6

3 tablespoons olive oil

5 pounds beef oxtails, joints separated

Salt and freshly ground black pepper

2 medium onions, cut into 6 wedges each

10 cloves garlic, chopped

2 carrots, peeled and diced

1 leek, white part only, rinsed and diced

3 stalks celery, diced

½ bunch Italian parsley, chopped

1 can (28 ounces) stewed tomatoes

1 can (28 ounces) tomato sauce

¼ cup balsamic vinegar

2 teaspoons sugar

1 teaspoon red pepper flakes

2 bay leaves

3 tablespoons Italian seasoning

2 teaspoons onion powder

2 teaspoons garlic powder

2 teaspoons dried oregano

SLOW-ROASTED BABY BACK RIBS

MARTY VERHAEG, ENGINE 13

"Low and slow" is the key to these easy, meltingly tender ribs that taste like something you'd get at an old-fashioned neighborhood barbecue joint. The other secret: Marty's spice rub. There's a 4-foot-long shelf in the kitchen at Station 13 that's packed with restaurant-size spice containers. Marty experimented with just about every one until he finally came up with this "red, white, and green" seasoning blend. If you start making the barbecue sauce as soon as the ribs go in, it'll be ready just in time to brush on at the end. Serve with Green Chile and Cheese Cornbread (page 181).

Adjust the oven rack to the center position and preheat the oven to 225°F. Lightly oil 2 rimmed baking sheets.

To make the Spice Rub: Combine the parsley, thyme, oregano, paprika, garlic salt, onion salt, sugar, and pepper in a small bowl.

To cook the ribs: If necessary, cut the rib slabs in half so that they can be arranged to fit on the baking sheets. Pat the spice rub onto the slabs, coating them all over as thoroughly as possible. Put the slabs on the baking sheets and roast them for 2 1/2 hours, turning them over twice during cooking. Remove the ribs from the oven and baste both sides of each slab with the barbecue sauce. Return to the oven and roast until the sauce is glazed and just beginning to brown, about 15 minutes. Slice the slabs into individual ribs and serve warm.

Serves 4 to 6

SPICE RUB

1 tablespoon dried parsley

1 tablespoon dried thyme

1 tablespoon dried oregano

1 tablespoon dried paprika

1 tablespoon garlic salt

1 tablespoon onion salt

1 tablespoon sugar

1 teaspoon freshly ground black pepper

2 slabs baby back pork ribs (about 4 pounds total)

1 to 2 cups Fireboat BBQ Sauce (page 102) or store-bought sauce

KALUA PIG

DAN BRIGHT, ENGINE 5

Dan grew up in Hawaii, where kalua pig (no relation to Kahlúa, the Mexican coffee liqueur) is a regular fixture at luaus. The real thing is made with a whole pig, roasted in a pit. This version, which Dan learned from a friend in Hawaii, requires just three ingredients and no shovel. It produces remarkably tender and succulent shredded pork, which Dan suggests serving with steamed rice. You can include it in a buffet, along with Kung Pao Prawns (page 124), Stanyan Street Fried Rice (page 173), and Napa Cabbage Salad (page 164). It also makes a fantastic filling for burritos.

Adjust the oven rack to the center position and preheat the oven to 400°F.

Cut several slashes in the pork, about ½ inch deep and 1½ inches long. Do not trim off the external fat. Brush the surface of the meat with the liquid smoke. Pat the salt evenly over the pork. Wrap the meat tightly in several layers of aluminum foil and put it in a heavy casserole dish or Dutch oven with a lid. Cover and bake for 4 hours.

Remove from the oven and carefully cut open the foil. The meat should be moist and falling apart. Allow it to cool slightly, then shred it with 2 forks.

Serves 6

1 boneless pork butt (about 4 pounds)

2 tablespoons liquid smoke

2 tablespoons kosher salt

SWOOP STEW

CURT NIELSEN, ENGINE 37

Every first-year "probie" assigned to Station 37 learns to make this easy, satisfying recipe, the invention of house manager and renowned cook, Curt "Swoop" Nielsen. It's a twist on the classic Italian combination of peppers and sausage, in which the sausages are formed into meatballs and simmered in a tomato sauce. Curt usually serves it over rice but also recommends trying it with pasta (a pound of penne will work well). When asked if 10 cloves of garlic might be a lot for six people, Curt laughs and says, "Not for six firefighters."

Roll the sausage meat into 1-inch balls between the palms of your hands.

Heat the olive oil in a large, heavy pot over medium heat. Add the sausage balls and sauté until evenly browned, about 5 minutes. Using a slotted spoon, remove the sausage balls, leaving as much fat in the pan as possible. Add the onions and garlic to the pan and sauté for 3 minutes. Add the mushrooms and sauté for 3 minutes more. Stir in the oregano, Italian seasoning, stewed tomatoes, and salsa. Return the sausage balls to the pot. Simmer, uncovered, for 15 minutes. Add the bell peppers and simmer until they are tender, about 20 minutes. Season to taste with salt and pepper.

While the stew simmers, cook the rice according to the package directions. Serve the stew hot over the rice.

Serves 6

2 pounds hot Italian sausages, casings removed

3 tablespoons olive oil

2 medium yellow onions, cut into 8 wedges each

10 cloves garlic, minced

1 pound mushrooms, sliced

3 tablespoons dried oregano

3 tablespoons Italian seasoning

1 can (28 ounces) stewed tomatoes

1 jar (16 ounces) tomato salsa

2 green bell peppers, stemmed, seeded, and thinly sliced

2 red bell peppers, stemmed, seeded, and thinly sliced

Salt and freshly ground black pepper

2 cups long-grain white rice

PORK MOLE

Theresa adapted this rich braised pork in a sweet-spicy mole sauce from a recipe she saw in the February 2002 issue of *Sunset* magazine. "It's perfect for the firehouse," she says, "because you throw everything in the pot and just let it cook." The extra step of browning the cooked meat in the oven at the end makes all the difference. This dish reheats well, so you can make it a day or two ahead of time.

Combine the onion, garlic, tomato, tomato juice, broth, brown sugar, vinegar, chipotle, dried chile, coriander, cloves, and cinnamon in a large, heavy-bottomed soup pot or Dutch oven with a tight-fitting lid. Put the pork in the pot. (The pot should be small enough that the pork should be at least half submerged in liquid.)

Place the pot over medium-high heat and bring to a boil; reduce the heat to low, cover, and simmer gently until the meat is tender when pierced with a fork, 3 to 3 1/2 hours. Stir the sauce and turn the meat occasionally while it is cooking.

Adjust the oven rack to the center position and preheat the oven to 350°F. Carefully transfer the meat in one piece to a foil-lined roasting pan, leaving the sauce in the pot. Bake the meat until it is well browned, 30 to 40 minutes.

Meanwhile, skim and discard the fat from the reserved sauce. Boil the sauce over high heat until it is reduced to 2 1/2 cups, 10 to 20 minutes. Purée the sauce in a blender or food processor until it is smooth; return it to the pot and keep warm. The sauce should have a thick consistency; if it is thin, continue to reduce it over medium-high heat. Season the sauce with salt and pepper to taste.

Remove the pork from the oven and slice it crosswise into 3 or 4 pieces. Using 2 forks, tear the meat into large chunks. Place the pork in a serving bowl and ladle the sauce over it. Garnish with the cilantro sprigs.

Serves 6

1 medium white onion, chopped

4 cloves garlic, peeled

1 ripe tomato, chopped

1 1/2 cups tomato juice

3/4 cup chicken broth

2 tablespoons brown sugar

3 tablespoons distilled white vinegar

1 tablespoon chopped canned chipotle chiles *en adobo*

1 dried ancho or pasilla chile, stemmed, seeded, deveined, and torn into pieces

1/2 teaspoon ground coriander

1/4 teaspoon ground cloves

1/4 teaspoon ground cinnamon

1 boneless pork butt roast (about 3 pounds), trimmed of external fat

Salt and freshly ground black pepper

Cilantro sprigs for garnish

Serve immediately with the tortillas, rice, and beans, passing the lime wedges at the table to squeeze over the pork.

Warming Tortillas: *Put up to 12 stacked tortillas in a plastic bag or wrap them in a barely damp kitchen towel. Put the tortillas in the microwave and heat on high power for 30 seconds to 2 minutes, depending on the number of tortillas. Let the tortillas sit for 3 to 4 minutes before unwrapping. To warm tortillas in the oven, wrap them in foil and put them in a 300°F oven for 10 to 15 minutes.*

ACCOMPANIMENTS

12 corn tortillas, warmed
Mexican Red Rice (page 174)
Pinto Beans with Garlic (page 175)
1 lime, cut into 6 wedges

MOM'S TAMALES

BOB LOPEZ, TRUCK 9

Tamales are more than a recipe. They're a social event. The more people you involve, the more tamales you can make—and the more fun you have. Bob's mom and dad, Mary and Ray, think nothing of rounding up family, friends, and strangers and turning out a thousand tamales in an afternoon for celebrations and fund-raisers at their church. So one day, Bob invited his parents to share their tamale-making talents with the crew at Station 9. They showed up at noon with a 25-pound tub of masa dough in hand. Mary made the filling, Ray got the husks ready, and everyone else just did what Mary told them to. By 5:00, 150 plump tamales were steaming up the kitchen windows. And Mary and Ray had made 14 new friends.

Start preparing the meat filling several hours ahead of time: Put the pork, garlic, and salt in a large Dutch oven. Add enough water to cover by 2 inches and bring to a boil over high heat. Reduce the heat, partially cover, and simmer for 2 hours, skimming off any scum from the surface during the first 30 minutes of cooking. Stir in the cumin, chili powder, and cornstarch mixture. Continue to simmer for 45 minutes, until the sauce has thickened. Remove from the heat and let cool for 2 hours.

Meanwhile, put the corn husks in a bowl and pour boiling water over them to cover. Weight them with a plate and let them soak for 2 to 3 hours, until soft. Remove the husks from the water and pat dry with a kitchen towel. Select 20 of the largest (at least 6 inches across at the wide end) and most pliable husks and set the others aside to use for lining the steamer. Tear 2 of the larger husks lengthwise into 1/4-inch strips for tying the tamales.

continued on page 77

Makes 18 tamales

2 pounds boneless lean pork butt, cut into 1/2-inch cubes

6 cloves garlic, chopped

2 tablespoons salt

1 tablespoon ground cumin

3 tablespoons chili powder, preferably Gebhardt's

3 tablespoons cornstarch dissolved in 1 cup water or chicken broth

About 36 corn husks (purchase an 8-ounce bag)

2 1/2 to 3 pounds prepared fresh masa dough for tamales (see Note, page 77)

ACCOMPANIMENTS

Pinto Beans with Garlic (page 175)

Mexican Red Rice (page 174)

When Bob decided to remodel his home kitchen, he turned to some colleagues from the department for a hand. "It's like your family," he says. "We help each other out in all kinds of ways."

Lay one of the remaining 18 corn husks on the work surface with the narrow end closest to you. Spread 2½ to 3 tablespoons of the masa dough on the widest part of the husk to form a square, leaving a border of 1½ inches at the wide end and about 3 inches at the narrow end. Spread 2 tablespoons of the filling in a line running up the center of the dough. Fold the sides of the husk in so that the filling is completely enclosed in dough, overlapping the sides of the husk slightly. Press gently along the seam to seal. Fold up the narrow end and fold the wider end down over it. Secure the tamale by tying one of the corn-husk strips around the center. Repeat with the remaining 17 husks.

To cook the tamales, fill the bottom of a steamer (or a large pot fitted with a steamer basket) with 4 to 5 inches of water. Set the steamer basket in place and line the bottom and sides of the basket with corn husks. Stack the tamales upright in the steamer so that they fit snugly but are not packed too tightly. Cover the tamales with more corn husks and place a clean kitchen towel over the top to prevent the condensation from the lid from dripping onto the tamales. Cover the steamer and bring to a simmer over medium heat. Allow the tamales to steam for 2 hours, checking the water level in the bottom from time to time and adding more boiling water as needed. Serve the tamales warm with beans and rice on the side.

Note: Fresh, ready-to-use masa dough for tamales—*masa preparada para tamales*—is sold in plastic tubs or bags in the refrigerator section of some Mexican markets and at some small, local tortilla factories.

JUNKYARD DOG CHAMPION CHILI

LT. MIKE PAPERA, ENGINE 48

Everyone knows firefighters take their chili seriously, but, for Mike, the subject is practically a religion. Back in the '80s, he helped organize a chili team to represent the department in cook-offs, and this recipe won them numerous awards throughout the state, including a first prize three years in a row in the SFFD cook-off. Since then, Mike has tasted his share of chilis as a judge for the International Chili Society, and he still considers this version the gold standard. "It's got lots of flavor, no beans, and it's not gonna bite you with too much heat," he says. "Serve it with a salad and some cornbread, and you've got yourself a winner."

Warm the oil in a large, heavy-bottomed soup pot or Dutch oven over medium heat. Working in batches, lightly brown the flank steak in the oil for about 4 minutes per batch. Use a slotted spoon to transfer the meat to a bowl. When all of the flank steak has been browned and removed, add the ground pork and sausage meat to the pot. Lightly brown the mixture, breaking up any large pieces with a spoon. Transfer to the bowl with the flank steak and set aside.

Add the onions, garlic, bell peppers, and jalapeños to the pot and sauté for 5 minutes. Stir in the chili powder, cumin, pepper, oregano, salt, paprika, cayenne, sugar, and bay leaf. Sauté for about 1 minute.

Serves 6

¼ cup canola oil

2 pounds flank steak, fat trimmed, cut into ¼-inch dice

1 pound coarsely ground pork

8 ounces mild Italian sausage, casings removed

8 ounces hot Italian sausage, casings removed

2 medium white onions, diced

4 cloves garlic, peeled

1 red bell pepper, seeded, and diced

1 green bell pepper, seeded, and diced

1 to 2 jalapeño chiles, seeded, and chopped

½ cup chili powder, preferably Gebhardt's

1 tablespoon ground cumin

1½ teaspoons freshly ground black pepper

1 teaspoon ground oregano

1 teaspoon salt

Add the stewed tomatoes, tomato sauce, salsa, chiles, broth, beer, and browned meat. Bring to a boil, then reduce to a gentle simmer and cook the chili over low heat, uncovered, for 2¹/₂ to 3 hours, stirring from time to time.

When ready to serve, skim off any excess fat from the surface of the chili and discard the bay leaf. Ladle into warm bowls and pass the sour cream, cheese, cilantro, green onions, and radishes at the table.

¹/₂ teaspoon paprika

¹/₄ teaspoon cayenne pepper

¹/₂ teaspoon sugar

1 bay leaf

1 can (28 ounces) Mexican-style stewed tomatoes

1 can (28 ounces) tomato sauce

1 cup green chile salsa

2 poblano chiles, roasted (see page 141), stemmed, seeded, and diced

1 cup beef broth

1 cup beer

ACCOMPANIMENTS

1 cup sour cream

1 cup grated Cheddar cheese

1 cup cilantro leaves

1 cup sliced green onions

1 cup thinly sliced red radishes

CHILI VERDE

BOB LOPEZ, TRUCK 9

Bob's mom taught him how to make this simple, satisfying pork and tomatillo chili. The best way to enjoy it is soft-taco style, wrapped in a fresh, warm corn tortilla with a dollop of sour cream and a sprig or two of cilantro.

Peel and discard the papery husks from the tomatillos and rinse them under cold water. Heat a large skillet over high heat and "toast" the tomatillos whole until they are lightly browned, about 5 minutes. Transfer them to a food processor or blender and purée. Set aside.

Heat the oil in a large, heavy-bottomed soup pot or Dutch oven with a tight-fitting lid. Add the pork and brown it on all sides. Stir in the chiles and garlic; sauté for 3 minutes. Stir in the tomatillo purée and salt. Bring the mixture to a boil, then reduce the heat to low and cover with the lid. Cook at a low simmer for 2 hours, stirring occasionally. Season with additional salt, if needed. Serve hot with the tortillas, sour cream, cilantro, rice, and beans.

Serves 6

1 pound tomatillos

3 tablespoons canola oil

3 pounds boneless pork butt, cut into 1-inch cubes

2 fresh jalapeño chiles, stemmed, seeded, and chopped

5 cloves garlic, minced

$1/2$ teaspoon salt

ACCOMPANIMENTS

Corn tortillas, warmed (see page 73)

Sour cream

Cilantro sprigs

Mexican Red Rice (page 174)

Pinto Beans with Garlic (page 175) or "Smoke and Fire" Black Beans (page 176)

RED GUMBO

Worthy is a native of Louisiana, and he remembers how his mother and grandmother would make their red gumbos with squirrel or rabbit. Now that he's a Californian—and a firehouse cook—Worthy opts for boneless chicken. Unlike some gumbos, this one is not thickened with a roux, so it's more like a hearty, tomatoey soup. Filé, a traditional Creole seasoning and thickener made from ground sassafras leaves, can be found in specialty groceries or in the spice section of many supermarkets.

In a large, heavy soup pot or Dutch oven with a tight-fitting lid, fry the bacon over medium heat until golden brown, about 4 minutes. Using a slotted spoon, transfer the bacon to a plate lined with paper towels and set aside. Add the hot links to the pot and brown them lightly for 3 to 4 minutes. Transfer to the plate with the bacon. Add the okra to the pot and fry until lightly browned, about 3 minutes; set aside on a separate plate.

Discard all but 2 tablespoons of fat from the pot. Add the garlic, onion, celery, and bell peppers and sauté for 5 minutes. Stir in the tomato sauce, diced tomatoes, water, chicken, Worcestershire sauce, Tabasco sauce, chili powder, and paprika. Return the bacon and hot links to the pot. Bring to a boil, then reduce the heat to low and simmer for 30 minutes.

Cook the rice according to the package directions and keep warm.

Add the okra, filé, parsley, prawns, and crab pieces to the pot, stirring to combine. Add the clams, discarding any that are broken or that are open and do not close when touched. Cover and cook over medium heat for 10 minutes, until the prawns are cooked through and the clams have opened. Discard any clams that are not open. Season to taste with salt and pepper and serve in large bowls, ladled over the rice.

Serves 6

8 ounces thick-cut bacon, diced

12 ounces hot link sausages, cut into
 1/2-inch pieces

1 pound okra, cut into 1/2-inch pieces

4 cloves garlic, chopped

1 yellow onion, diced

1 stalk celery, diced

1 red bell pepper, stemmed, seeded,
 and diced

1 green bell pepper, stemmed, seeded,
 and diced

1 can (28 ounces) tomato sauce

1 can (28 ounces) diced tomatoes

2 cups water

1 pound boneless, skinless chicken
 breasts, cut into 1-inch cubes

2 tablespoons Worcestershire sauce

1 tablespoon Tabasco sauce

1 tablespoon chili powder

2 teaspoons paprika

2 cups white rice

Preparing Cooked Crab: *To clean cooked crab, use a small knife or screwdriver to open the tailpiece on the belly side. Pull it away from the body, separating it completely. Pry off and discard the upper shell and remove the jellylike substance under it. Cut the body into quarters, discarding the gills, intestines, and "sandbags." Rinse the crab pieces under cold running water.*

1 tablespoon filé

⅓ cup chopped parsley

1 pound medium prawns, peeled and deveined

2 cooked Dungeness crabs, cleaned and quartered

2 pounds Manila or littleneck clams, scrubbed

Salt and freshly ground black pepper

VILLA GUMBO

RICH GIBSON, ENGINE 37

Station 37 is one of the city's oldest firehouses. Its stately 1915 façade has earned it the nickname "The Villa." It's a house with many long-standing traditions, and Rich—who's worked there for more than 30 years—is proud to count his famous gumbo among them.

To prepare the roux: Heat the oil in a large, heavy-bottomed soup pot or Dutch oven over medium-low heat and sprinkle in the flour. Cook, stirring constantly, until the roux is a nutty brown color, 10 to 15 minutes.

Add the yellow onion and garlic to the roux; cook for 3 minutes. Add the tomatoes, bell peppers, green onions, and parsley; cook for 10 minutes. Add the broth, cloves, thyme, mace, cayenne, bay leaves, lemon juice, okra, fish, hot links, and chicken. Bring to a boil, then reduce the heat to low and simmer for 30 minutes. Add the prawns and simmer for 15 minutes. Discard the bay leaves and season to taste with salt and pepper. Allow the gumbo to rest for 10 minutes before serving.

Meanwhile, cook the rice according to the package directions. Serve the gumbo over the rice.

Serves 6

½ cup oil

½ cup all-purpose flour

1 large yellow onion, diced

5 cloves garlic, chopped

1 can (28 ounces) diced tomatoes, drained

1 green bell pepper, seeded, and diced

1 red bell pepper, seeded, and diced

6 green onions, chopped

½ cup chopped parsley

6 cups chicken broth or water

½ teaspoon ground cloves

1 tablespoon dried thyme

½ teaspoon ground mace

1 teaspoon cayenne pepper

2 bay leaves

1 tablespoon freshly squeezed lemon juice

8 ounces okra, sliced

1 pound firm white fish fillets, such as cod or sea bass, cut into cubes

12 ounces hot link sausages, sliced

1 pound boneless, skinless chicken breasts, cut into cubes

1 pound medium prawns, peeled and deveined

Salt and freshly ground black pepper

2 cups white rice

TAMALE PIE

TOM MARINI, ENGINE 39

Tom's wife, Marguerite, gave him this classic American recipe to make for the crew at Station 39. It's a great one for a potluck or a big group meal, because it's easy, travels and holds well, and feeds a lot of people.

Heat the olive oil in a large, heavy-bottomed soup pot or Dutch oven over medium heat and sauté the onion until translucent, about 5 minutes. Add the ground beef and sausage. Cook for 5 minutes or until browned, stirring to break up any large pieces. Using a large spoon, remove and discard as much of the fat as possible from the pan. Sprinkle in the chili powder and taco seasoning and cook for 1 minute, stirring. Stir in the tomato sauce and beef broth. Reduce the heat to low and simmer for 30 minutes. Stir in the olives and corn. Season to taste with salt and pepper.

Meanwhile, put the chicken broth in a large saucepan, bring it to a boil, and whisk in the cornmeal. Reduce the heat and cook, stirring frequently, until thick, about 20 minutes. Season to taste with salt.

Adjust the oven rack to the center position and preheat the oven to 350°F. Lightly oil a 9-by-13-inch baking pan.

When the cornmeal is cooked, spoon it into the baking pan and ladle the ground beef mixture on top. Use a wooden spoon to stir some of the ground beef into the cornmeal. Top with the cheese, if using. Bake for 30 minutes.

Serves 6

2 tablespoons olive oil

1 medium yellow onion, diced

1 pound lean ground beef

8 ounces hot Italian sausage, casings removed

2 teaspoons chili powder

1 package (1 1/4 ounces) taco seasoning mix

1 can (8 ounces) tomato sauce

1 cup beef broth

1 can pitted black olives (drained weight 6 to 7 ounces), drained

1 package (10 ounces) frozen corn kernels, thawed

Salt and freshly ground black pepper

4 cups chicken broth

1 cup yellow cornmeal

1 cup grated sharp Cheddar cheese (optional)

CHICKEN and PORK POZOLE

LARRY CANNON, ENGINE 29

Pozole is a hearty Mexican dish that gets its distinctive flavor from hominy—the dried, hulled field corn used to make tortillas and tamales. You can find dried hominy (also referred to as *pozole* or *posole* on the package) in Hispanic markets and many supermarkets. It looks like very large popcorn kernels. You can also buy precooked, canned hominy, which has less flavor than the dried kind. If you go that route, substitute one 28-ounce can of hominy, drained and rinsed, for the 8 ounces of dried hominy in this recipe; reduce the simmering time to 1 hour and add the hominy during the last 30 minutes of cooking.

The night before: Put the hominy in a large bowl with enough water to cover and let it soak overnight.

The next day: Drain the hominy in a colander and rinse under cold water. Lightly season the pork with salt and pepper. Heat the olive oil in a large, heavy-bottomed soup pot or Dutch oven with a lid over medium heat; add the pork and brown on all sides for about 5 minutes. Remove the pork with a slotted spoon and set it aside. Add the chicken to the pot and sauté until it is lightly browned, about 3 minutes. Remove the chicken and set it aside with the pork.

Add the onion and garlic to the pot and sauté for about 2 minutes. Stir in the chili powder, oregano, and cumin. Add the soaked hominy and the chicken broth. Bring to a boil, then reduce the heat to low, partially cover the pot, and simmer, stirring from time to time, for 1 hour, until the hominy is tender. Return the pork and chicken to the pot, along with any of the meat juices. Simmer for 1 to 1½ hours more, uncovered, until the meat is tender. Season to taste with salt and pepper.

Serves 6 to 8

8 ounces (1½ cups) dried hominy

8 ounces boneless pork loin, cut into ½-inch cubes

Salt and freshly ground black pepper

2 tablespoons olive oil

1 pound boneless, skinless chicken thighs, cut into ½-inch cubes

1 medium yellow onion, diced

2 cloves garlic, minced

1 tablespoon mild chili powder

1 tablespoon dried Mexican oregano

1 teaspoon ground cumin

7 cups chicken broth

To serve, put the cilantro, cabbage, green onions, radishes, jalapeños, and lime wedges in separate bowls. Ladle the warm pozole into bowls and serve with the warm tortillas, letting everyone top their pozole with the accompaniments of their choice.

ACCOMPANIMENTS

½ bunch cilantro, stems removed

2 cups shredded green cabbage

6 green onions, white and pale green parts only, chopped

8 radishes, thinly sliced

4 roasted jalapeño chiles (see page 141), stemmed, seeded, and chopped

2 limes, cut into wedges

12 corn tortillas, warmed (see page 73)

MATT'S SAUERKRAUT SAUSAGE SURPRISE

MATT TARLACH, ENGINE 48

"The surprise? It's good!" says Matt. He's right. This is a substantial meat-and-potatoes dish that's made in a single pot. Matt got this recipe from a French roommate, who called it Choucroute Royale, but he's changed some things about it over the years, including the name, which, he notes, was "much too fancy for the firehouse."

In a large, heavy-bottomed soup pot or Dutch oven with a tight-fitting lid, lightly sauté the bacon over medium heat until it is just beginning to brown, about 4 minutes. Using a slotted spoon, transfer the bacon to a plate and set aside. Lightly brown the sausage pieces in the bacon fat for about 3 minutes and transfer them to the plate with the bacon. Season the pork chops with salt and pepper and brown them in the bacon fat for 1 to 2 minutes per side. Transfer them to a separate plate.

Put the onion and garlic in the pot and sauté for 5 minutes. Stir in the juniper berries, savory, caraway seeds, and bay leaf. Sauté for 1 minute. Add the sauerkraut, potatoes, bacon, and sausage, then stir in the chicken broth and brown sugar. Bring to a simmer and layer the pork chops over the surface. Cover the pot and simmer over low heat for 30 minutes. Scatter the apples over the pork chops. Cover and simmer for about 20 minutes, or until the potatoes and apples are tender.

To serve, arrange the pork chops around the edge of a large platter. Discard the bay leaf, mound the sauerkraut mixture in the center of the platter, and drizzle the pan juices over all. Pass the mustard and applesauce at the table.

Serves 6

4 ounces thick-cut bacon, cut into
    1/4-inch pieces

1 pound smoked sausage (such as
    kielbasa or smoked bratwurst), cut
    on the diagonal into 2-inch pieces

6 boneless pork chops, 3/4 inch thick

Salt and freshly ground black pepper

1 medium yellow onion, halved and
    thinly sliced

1 clove garlic, sliced

4 juniper berries, crushed

1 teaspoon dried savory

1 teaspoon caraway seeds, crushed

1 bay leaf

1 jar (22 ounces) sauerkraut

1 pound small Yukon Gold potatoes,
    halved

1 cup chicken broth

1 tablespoon brown sugar

3 medium green apples, peeled, cored,
    and cut into chunks

ACCOMPANIMENTS

Stone-ground mustard

Applesauce

SKILLET PAELLA

DARRYL DAIR, TRUCK 11

This paella is a bit soupier than the traditional Spanish version, so Darryl recommends serving it with a good loaf of French bread to take care of any extra broth left in the bowl. If fresh crab isn't easy to come by where you live, try substituting a pound or two of large, uncooked prawns in the shell.

Season the chicken with salt and pepper. In a large, cast-iron skillet or Dutch oven with a tight-fitting lid, heat the oil over medium-high heat and lightly brown the chicken on all sides for 3 to 4 minutes. Transfer the chicken to a plate using tongs or a slotted spoon. Add the sausage to the skillet and cook until golden brown. Remove and let cool; slice into 1-inch pieces. Add the onion, celery, bell pepper, and garlic to the skillet and sauté for 4 minutes over medium heat. Add the rice, stirring to coat the grains in the oil for 1 minute. Stir in the tomatoes (with their liquid), saffron infusion, broth, chicken, and sausage. Cover and cook for 20 minutes over low heat.

Arrange the crab pieces around the edge of the pan and layer the clams on top, discarding any that are broken or that are open and do not close when touched. Cover and cook over medium heat until the clams have opened, about 5 minutes. Discard any that have not opened. Season with salt and pepper. Garnish with the parsley and serve directly from the skillet.

Serves 6

3 boneless, skinless chicken thighs, cut into 2-inch pieces

Salt and freshly ground black pepper

¼ cup olive oil

1 pound hot Italian sausage

1 medium yellow onion, diced

1 stalk celery, chopped

1 red or green bell pepper, stemmed, seeded, and cut into ¼-inch slices

2 cloves garlic, chopped

2½ cups long-grain converted rice

1 can (14½ ounces) diced tomatoes in purée

½ teaspoon saffron threads, crushed and steeped in 3 tablespoons hot chicken broth

6 cups chicken broth

2 cooked Dungeness crabs, cleaned and quartered (see page 83)

2 pounds Manila or littleneck clams, scrubbed

¼ cup chopped parsley for garnish

CALIFORNIA CHICKEN ADOBO   LARRY ABELLA, TRUCK 9

When he was a little kid, Larry asked his mom to show him how to make his favorite Filipino dish, adobo—a chicken stew that tastes a little like teriyaki, only tangier—and he's been making it ever since. The ginger is his own "California addition," and he notes that you can also make this recipe with pork short ribs or a combination of chicken and pork. "The vinegar is the key to the whole thing," he says. "When I get a craving for that vinegar taste, I just have to get in the kitchen and make adobo." At the firehouse, he tends to balance the vinegar with a little extra brown sugar or a few spoonfuls of bottled teriyaki sauce right before serving.

Heat the vinegar and soy sauce in a large, heavy-bottomed soup pot or Dutch oven with a tight-fitting lid over medium-high heat. Add the onion, garlic, paprika, garlic powder, onion powder, bay leaves, ginger, and peppercorns. Season to taste with salt. Put the chicken in the pot, stirring to coat it well. Bring to a boil, then immediately lower the heat, cover, and simmer for 30 minutes. Uncover the pot and simmer for 15 minutes more, or until the sauce is reduced by half. Add brown sugar to taste. Discard the bay leaves.

Meanwhile, cook the rice according to the package directions. Serve the adobo with the rice.

Serves 4 to 6

1/3 cup distilled white vinegar

1/2 cup soy sauce

1/2 yellow onion, sliced

5 cloves garlic, chopped

1/2 teaspoon paprika

1/4 teaspoon garlic powder

1/4 teaspoon onion powder

3 bay leaves

1 piece fresh ginger, about 1 inch long, peeled and minced

1 tablespoon peppercorns

Salt

3 pounds bone-in chicken thighs, skin removed

1 to 2 tablespoons brown sugar

2 cups white rice

CHICKEN IN A BARREL

Where do you find the best chicken in San Francisco? Hint: It's not at a restaurant. No, the crispiest, juiciest, tastiest chicken in the city is at Station 35 on the Embarcadero.

Out back, on the dock overlooking the Bay Bridge, fireboat pilot Bob Costa has rigged up a slow-cooker made from an oil drum and some recycled barbecue parts. It doesn't look like much, but the chicken it produces is justifiably famous in the department.

Bob commutes to work from the tiny town of Murphys in Calaveras County—the heart of gold rush country—where he and his wife run a bed-and-breakfast, Dunbar House, 1880. Communal Chicken in a Barrel dinners have been a summertime attraction in Murphys for more than thirty years, and Bob fabricates the barrel cookers in his home welding shop.

The cooking process could hardly be simpler. Six chickens are split in half, marinated in olive oil, lemon juice, and seasonings, and hung on hooks high above the smoldering coals. "Then you just close the lid and forget about it," says Bob with a shrug. "No basting, no turning, and definitely no peeking." The barrel maintains an even temperature of 350°F and just the right combination of moisture and smoke for about an hour and a half—enough time to cook the chickens perfectly. "Then it basically starts turning itself down automatically," Bob adds. "If we get a call while the chicken's cooking, we just leave it. It's impossible to overcook." And once you've tasted it, it's impossible to forget.

Chicken in a Barrel really can't be made without the barrel, but you can turn out a tasty approximation on a home grill with a cover. Cut a frying chicken in half lengthwise and coat it with a mixture of 2 tablespoons olive oil and 2 tablespoons lemon juice. Using enough coals to cover half of the bottom of the grill (about 4 pounds for a typical large round grill), prepare a medium-hot fire (see page 99). Push the coals to one side and place a foil-lined 9-by-13-inch metal baking pan next to them. Rub the chicken with a mixture of $\frac{1}{2}$ teaspoon seasoned salt, $\frac{1}{2}$ teaspoon granulated garlic, $\frac{1}{2}$ teaspoon paprika, and $\frac{1}{2}$ teaspoon chopped dried rosemary. Set the grill rack in place and put the chicken halves, skin-side down, on the grate over the baking pan, making sure no part of the chicken is directly over the coals. Close the grill cover and open the vents. After 40 minutes, turn the chicken over, replace the cover, and cook for 30 to 40 minutes more, until the thighs release clear juices when pricked with a fork and an instant-read thermometer inserted in the thighs registers 175°F.

BUZ'S PERFECT FRIED CHICKEN BUZ ORENGO, TRUCK 48

Station 48 is a uniquely San Franciscan outpost in the middle of the Bay on Treasure Island—and Buz's famous fried chicken is one of the island's culinary treasures. His secret: the overnight marinade in a buttermilk brine makes the chicken moist, tender, and extra-tasty. Serve with a drizzle of honey and a big helping of Coleslaw with Pineapple and Dried Cherries (page 163).

Combine the buttermilk, evaporated milk, salt, and Tabasco in an airtight container large enough to hold the chicken pieces. Add the chicken and toss to coat. Refrigerate overnight.

Half an hour before you are ready to fry the chicken, remove it from the refrigerator and let it come to room temperature. Combine the flour, baking powder, white pepper, and cayenne in a large, resealable plastic bag. Remove the chicken pieces from the buttermilk mixture. One at a time put each piece in the bag with the flour mixture, seal the bag, and shake it until the chicken is evenly coated, then shake off any excess coating back into the bag.

Heat the vegetable shortening and bacon drippings, if using, in a large, deep-sided skillet or deep fryer until a candy/deep-fat thermometer registers 335°F. Fry the chicken pieces in batches, being sure not to crowd them. Cook until golden brown: 15 to 20 minutes for the breast pieces, 10 to 15 minutes for the thighs and drumsticks, and about 10 minutes for the wings. Using tongs, turn the pieces from time to time, being careful to keep the crust intact. Transfer the cooked pieces to a plate lined with several layers of paper towels. Serve warm, at room temperature, or cold.

Serves 6 to 8

4 cups buttermilk

1 can (12 ounces) unsweetened
    evaporated milk

¼ cup salt

3 tablespoons Tabasco sauce

2 frying chickens, cut up

3 cups all-purpose flour

2 tablespoons baking powder

1 tablespoon ground white pepper

1 teaspoon cayenne pepper

3 pounds vegetable shortening

¼ cup bacon drippings (optional)

BOB'S OVEN-FRIED CHICKEN

BOB IMBELLINO, ENGINE 13

This simple recipe has been passed from station to station throughout the city for years. It produces crispy, golden, moist "fried" chicken without the fat and mess of frying. It's equally good hot from the oven or at room temperature, making it a fine choice for a picnic.

Adjust the oven rack to the center position and preheat the oven to 400°F. Lightly grease two 9-by-13-inch rimmed baking sheets.

Combine the cornmeal, flour, ginger, salt, sugar, paprika, onion salt, and garlic salt in a large, resealable plastic bag. Pour the milk into a large bowl. One piece at a time, dip the chicken in the milk and put it in the bag with the cornmeal mixture. Seal the bag and shake it until the chicken is evenly coated, then shake off any excess coating back into the bag.

Put the breaded chicken on the baking sheets in a single layer with as much space between the pieces as possible. Bake until the chicken is deep golden brown and releases clear juices when pricked with a fork, 55 to 60 minutes.

Serves 6 to 8

1/2 cup cornmeal

1/2 cup all-purpose flour

2 teaspoons ground ginger

2 teaspoons salt

2 teaspoons sugar

2 teaspoons paprika

1 teaspoon onion salt

1 teaspoon garlic salt

2 cups low-fat milk

2 frying chickens, cut up

THAI BBQ CHICKEN
with PEANUT SAUCE

MIKE TIN, ENGINE 21

If you like the flavor of Thai chicken satay, give this amazingly authentic-tasting recipe a try. If grilling isn't convenient, you can make it in the broiler. You'll find tamarind paste sold in jars or cans in Asian or Indian specialty markets (you want the paste with no seeds, sometimes sold as tamarind concentrate). If it's not available, substitute the same amount of fresh lime juice. The marinade and dipping sauce also work well with beef and pork and will keep for several days in the refrigerator. Try tossing the dipping sauce with chilled cooked Chinese egg noodles, chopped peanuts, and minced green onions to make a cold peanut noodle salad.

To marinate the chicken: Whisk together the garlic, cilantro, fish sauce, pepper, curry powder, and coconut milk in a medium bowl. Put the chicken in a baking dish and pour the marinade over it, tossing to coat well. Cover and refrigerate for 3 to 4 hours.

To make the dipping sauce: In a medium saucepan, combine the curry paste, paprika, garlic, fish sauce, peanut butter, tamarind paste, brown sugar, peanuts, and coconut milk; simmer until the sauce is thickened and reduced by half, about 15 minutes. Serve warm or at room temperature.

Prepare the grill with a medium-hot fire (see page 99).

Cook the rice according to the package directions and keep warm.

Serves 6

MARINADE

2 tablespoons minced garlic

3 tablespoons chopped cilantro

1/4 cup Thai or Vietnamese fish sauce

1 teaspoon freshly ground black pepper

1 teaspoon curry powder

1 cup coconut milk

4 pounds bone-in chicken thighs

PEANUT DIPPING SAUCE

1 teaspoon Thai-style green curry paste (such as Thai Kitchen brand)

1 teaspoon paprika

1 teaspoon minced garlic

2 tablespoons Thai or Vietnamese fish sauce

2 tablespoons creamy peanut butter

1 tablespoon tamarind paste

To grill the chicken: Remove the chicken from the refrigerator 15 minutes before cooking. Drain off the excess marinade, reserving some for basting. Grill the chicken for 30 minutes, turning frequently and moving the pieces away from the hottest coals as needed to keep it from burning. Baste occasionally with the reserved marinade; do not baste during the last 10 minutes of cooking. When the thighs are cooked through, transfer them to a platter and garnish with the peanuts, cilantro, and lime wedges. Serve with the rice and pass the dipping sauce at the table.

3 tablespoons light brown sugar

¼ cup chopped roasted peanuts

2 cups coconut milk

2 cups jasmine or basmati rice

GARNISHES

Chopped roasted peanuts

Cilantro sprigs

1 lime, cut into 6 wedges

COOKING WITH FIRE

"We're out here every night in the summer," says firefighter Steve Feiner, pointing to the courtyard behind Station 16 in the Marina, where a gleaming new grill is parked under the hose-drying tower. "Come to think of it, we're out here a lot all year."

From Treasure Island to Chinatown, every firehouse in San Francisco has a grill—and every firehouse grill gets a workout. It's partly because grilling is such a good way to feed a big group. But it's more than that. "It's definitely a social thing," says Steve. "If one person's grilling, everybody comes out and helps. It's just an instant gathering spot—even more than the stove—where everybody can stand around and talk about the day."

And when you think about what these men and women do all day, is it any surprise that they're masters of the art of cooking with live fire?

Here are some tips for the next time you fire up the grill at your place.

Cleaning the Grill Rack

Clean the grill rack with a wire brush twice: once when you're finished cooking, while it's still hot, and again right before the next time you use it, to clean off any rust or debris.

Starting the Coals

Skip the lighter fluid and make a onetime investment in a sturdy chimney charcoal starter. Fill it with coals, pack some newspaper loosely into the bottom, and set it inside the barbecue with the grill rack removed. Light the newspaper and keep an eye on the coals to make sure the ones on the bottom have begun to glow. After about 15 minutes, the coals should be glowing bright red. Wearing a long oven mitt, carefully pick up the chimney and pour the coals out into the grill, using tongs to spread them out a bit. If you have a big grill and are cooking a lot of food, you can add more coals on top of the hot coals at this point. Now put the grill rack back in place and wait until the coals are uniformly covered with gray ash, 10 to 15 minutes more. If using a gas grill, preheat it for 15 minutes or more, following the manufacturer's directions.

Regulating the Heat

The heat of a charcoal fire can be regulated simply by mounding the coals or spreading them out. The more you spread them, the less intense their heat will be.

To gauge the heat of the fire, hold your hand palm down about 4 inches above the grill. If you can hold it there for only 2 to 3 seconds, you have a hot fire; 5 to 6 seconds means a medium-hot fire; 8 to 9 seconds indicates a low fire. Most meats, chicken, and fish cook best over a medium-hot fire. Arrange the coals so that you have a less-hot area where you can move pieces of food that are cooking too quickly. Vegetables generally cook best over a medium-low fire, so grill them last, once the coals have begun to die down.

Six Tools to Have on Hand

- Long-handled grilling spatula
- Long-handled grilling tongs
- Wire brush to clean the grill rack
- Spray bottle filled with water
- Flashlight, if grilling at night
- Fire extinguisher and/or box of baking soda to put out grease fires

Taming the Flames

Open flames are the enemy of food on the grill, causing it to char and creating an unpleasant smoky flavor. Most grilled foods need to cook gradually over ash-covered coals. But fat or basting sauces dripping from foods on the grill will inevitably cause flames to flare up. To minimize this, spray a small amount of water on the coals with a spray bottle and, if your grill has a lid, briefly cover it until the flames die down.

GRILLING MARINADES and SAUCES

"ANY KIND OF MEAT" MARINADE

STEVE MILLER, ENGINE 34

Steve got this recipe from a Filipina woman who worked with a friend of his in an Alaskan salmon cannery. He's had success using it on salmon, chicken, and "any kind of meat."

1 cup ketchup

1/4 cup Asian oyster sauce

2 tablespoons honey

2 tablespoons lemon juice

1 tablespoon soy sauce

Combine all the ingredients in a medium bowl. Marinate meat, poultry, or seafood for 2 hours or overnight.

Makes about 1 1/2 cups, enough for 2 1/2 pounds of meat, poultry, or seafood

YUCATÁN MARINADE

MIKE GUAJARDO, ENGINE 16

This tangy grilling marinade adds a lot of flavor to chicken, pork, prawns, scallops, or any firm-fleshed fish, such as snapper, sea bass, or salmon. If you use it with fish or shellfish, marinate them for no more than half an hour, as the citrus juice will "cook" the seafood.

Juice of 2 oranges (about 2/3 cup)

Juice of 2 limes (about 1/4 cup)

Juice of 2 lemons (about 6 tablespoons)

3 cloves garlic, minced

1 jalapeño chile, stemmed, seeded, and thinly sliced

1 teaspoon ground cumin

1/2 teaspoon cayenne

1 teaspoon dried oregano

1 teaspoon salt

Combine all the ingredients in a medium bowl. If using with poultry or pork, marinate for 3 to 4 hours before grilling.

Makes about 1 cup, enough for at least 3 pounds of poultry, meat, or seafood

HONEY-MUSTARD MARINADE

CHRISTINE WILLIAMS, ENGINE 21

Christine came up with this easy, big-flavored, fat-free marinade that's great for grilling—not to mention broiling or roasting. Try it on chicken, turkey breast, pork chops, or pork tenderloin.

3/4 cup honey

3/4 cup Dijon mustard

5 tablespoons soy sauce

3 tablespoons ground cumin

5 cloves garlic, chopped

Warm the honey in a small saucepan. Stir in the mustard, soy sauce, cumin, and garlic. Remove from the heat and let cool before using. Allow meat or poultry to marinate for at least 4 hours or overnight.

Makes about 1 3/4 cups, enough for 3 to 4 pounds of meat or poultry

FIREBOAT BBQ SAUCE

BILL WICKLIFFE, ENGINE 35

This classic barbecue sauce will keep for up to 2 weeks in the refrigerator. Baste it on grilled or roasted chicken, beef, or ribs during the last 5 to 10 minutes of cooking.

3 cups beef broth

1 can (6 ounces) tomato paste

1/2 cup Dijon mustard

1/2 cup Worcestershire sauce

1/4 cup white vinegar

1 cup brown sugar

2 tablespoons chili powder

1 tablespoon red pepper flakes

3 tablespoons liquid smoke

Combine all the ingredients in a medium, heavy saucepan and bring to a boil, stirring continuously. Reduce the heat to a simmer and cook for 2 hours. Remove from the heat and let cool before transferring to a storage container.

Makes 2 3/4 cups

POLYNESIAN BASTING SAUCE

LT. JOE HIGGINS, DIVISION OF TRAINING

Joe bastes this sauce on grilled or baked chicken during the last 5 minutes of cooking.

1 cup ketchup

½ teaspoon dry mustard

2 tablespoons brown sugar

1 can (8 ounces) pineapple chunks, drained

Combine the ketchup, dry mustard, and brown sugar. When the chicken is nearly done, baste with the ketchup mixture, put a few pineapple chunks on each piece of chicken, and continue to cook until the chicken is glazed, about 5 minutes.

Makes about 1 cup, enough for about 6 pounds of chicken

ED'S TARTAR SAUCE

LT. ED DEA, DIVISION OF TRAINING

There's an unspoken rule in the firehouse kitchen: If there's time, make it from scratch. It's a good rule to follow in the case of this fresh-tasting tartar sauce, which is great with fish or on sandwiches. Try it as a base for a quick potato salad, too.

¾ cup mayonnaise

1 teaspoon Dijon mustard

¼ teaspoon cayenne pepper

3 tablespoons finely chopped green onions, white and pale green parts only

3 tablespoons finely chopped parsley

1 tablespoon sweet pickle relish

In a small bowl, whisk together the mayonnaise, mustard, and cayenne. Stir in the green onions, parsley, and relish. Store in an airtight container, refrigerated, for up to 1 week.

Makes about 1 cup

CHICKEN and CHORIZO ENCHILADAS

BOB LOPEZ, TRUCK 9

Chicken enchiladas are a menu standby in the city's firehouses, and Bob's, made with fresh chorizo, are among the best. Look for Mexican pork chorizo in Hispanic markets. It's a spicy fresh sausage, not to be confused with the Spanish-style smoked or cured version.

To make the filling: Put the chicken in a large pot with a tight-fitting lid and add enough water to cover. Bring to a boil, then reduce the heat to medium and cover the pot. Simmer for 40 minutes, until the chicken is cooked through. Remove the chicken and let it rest until it is cool enough to handle. Skim the fat from the broth and reserve 2 cups of the broth to use in the sauce. (Save the remainder for another use.) Remove and discard the skin and bones from the chicken. Using your hands, shred the meat; transfer to a large bowl. In a large skillet, sauté the chorizo over medium heat, breaking up any large pieces, for 2 minutes. Add the onion, garlic, and celery and sauté with the chorizo for 4 minutes. Pour the mixture into the bowl with the shredded chicken. Add the oregano and olives and stir to combine well. Let the filling cool to room temperature.

To make the enchilada sauce: While the filling is cooling, heat the oil in a medium saucepan (choose one that will be large enough to accommodate a tortilla when it is dipped in the sauce) over medium heat and stir in the flour to make a roux. Cook until the roux is the color of peanut butter, about 5 minutes. Stir in the chili powder. Whisk in the 2 cups reserved chicken broth and bring to a boil, whisking continuously until smooth. Reduce the heat to low and simmer for 10 minutes. Season to taste with salt and pepper. Keep warm.

Serves 4 to 6

FILLING

1 whole frying chicken

1 pound fresh pork chorizo sausage, casings removed

1 medium yellow onion, diced

2 cloves garlic, minced

2 stalks celery, diced

1 tablespoon dried oregano, preferably Mexican

1/2 cup sliced black olives

ENCHILADA SAUCE

2 tablespoons vegetable oil

2 tablespoons all-purpose flour

6 tablespoons mild chili powder (such as Gebhardt's)

Salt and freshly ground black pepper

1/3 cup vegetable oil

12 corn tortillas

2 cups grated cheese, a mixture of Cheddar and Jack

ACCOMPANIMENTS

Pinto Beans with Garlic (page 175)

Mexican Red Rice (page 174)

Bob learned to cook from his mother, Mary, "who never measures anything," and he's already working on handing everything he learned from her down to the next generation. He's accumulating all the recipes he cooks at the firehouse to make a family cookbook for his kids.

Adjust the oven rack to the center position and preheat the oven to 350°F. Lightly oil a 9-by-13-inch baking pan.

To assemble the enchiladas: Heat the oil in a large skillet over medium heat. Using tongs, lightly fry the tortillas in the oil, one at a time, for about 10 seconds on each side to soften them; drain the tortillas on several layers of paper towels. Dip one tortilla in the warm enchilada sauce; let the excess sauce drip back into the saucepan and place the tortilla on a clean work surface. Put about 1/2 cup of the filling and about 1 1/2 tablespoons of the cheese in a line along the bottom third of the tortilla. Roll the tortilla around the filling and place it in the baking pan, seam-side down. Fill and roll the remaining tortillas in the same way, lining them up in the baking dish in a single layer. Spoon the remaining enchilada sauce over the top and sprinkle with the remaining cheese. Bake until the enchiladas are heated through and the cheese is melted and bubbly, about 20 minutes. Serve the enchiladas warm with the beans and rice on the side.

CHICKEN RELLENO

CANTREZ TRIPLITT, ENGINE 37

As entrées go, this Filipino-style stuffed boneless chicken is on the ambitious side. But it's also on the delicious side, and it's fun to serve at a dinner party, because it looks like a beautiful roast chicken, but when carved, it reveals a savory rice, pork, and mushroom filling. You can also roast it a day ahead of time, refrigerate it overnight, and serve it as a cold entrée, in which case, as Cantrez says, "It'll slice just like a meatloaf."

To make the stuffing: Heat the oil in a large skillet over medium heat and lightly brown the sausage and pork for about 3 minutes, stirring to break up any large pieces. Add the mushrooms, green onions, bell pepper, garlic, and soy sauce. Sauté until the pepper is tender, about 8 minutes. In a large bowl, combine the sausage mixture with the cooked rice. Season to taste with salt and pepper; allow the mixture to cool completely.

To debone the chicken: Place the chicken on a work surface, breast-side down. Using poultry shears, cut along both sides of the backbone, as close to the bone as possible. Remove and discard the backbone. Open the chicken and flatten it with the palms of your hands. Pull out the central breast bone with your fingers and discard it. Using a sharp boning or paring knife, cut out and discard the central rib of cartilage and the wishbone. Carefully cut away the main breast bone and ribs on both sides. Leave the wing bones intact. Starting at the end of the thigh bone closest to the back, use the knife to scrape the meat away from one of the thigh bones so that the bone protrudes. When you reach the knee joint, continue to cut and scrape around it and down the leg, further

Serves 4 to 6

2 teaspoons vegetable oil

4 ounces hot Italian sausage, casings removed

4 ounces ground pork

4 ounces mushrooms, sliced

3 green onions, white and pale green parts only, chopped

½ red bell pepper, stemmed, seeded, and diced

1 clove garlic, minced

1 tablespoon soy sauce

1½ cups cooked long-grain white rice

Salt and freshly ground black pepper

1 whole frying chicken (3½ to 4 pounds)

2 tablespoons butter, melted

Paprika

exposing the bone, until you reach the knuckle. Reinsert the thigh-leg bone. With the back of the blade of a chef's knife, strike the outside of the leg just above the knuckle to break the bone inside without cutting through the skin. You should now be able to pull out the thigh-leg bone in one piece, leaving the knuckle intact. Repeat with the other thigh-leg bone.

Adjust the oven rack to the center position and preheat the oven to 350°F.

To stuff the chicken: Lay the chicken on the work surface, skin-side down, and pack a small amount of the stuffing into the cavities inside the legs and thighs. Spread the rest of the stuffing over the breast area. Depending on the size of the bird, you may not need all of the stuffing. Do not overstuff the chicken, as this may cause it to burst when cooking. Fold the chicken around the stuffing so that the cut edges of the back meet. Secure with toothpicks. Carefully turn the chicken breast-side up and mold it with your hands so that it takes on its original shape. Rub the chicken all over with the butter and season it with salt, pepper, and paprika.

Transfer the chicken to a roasting pan and put it in the oven, immediately lowering the temperature to 325°F. Cook until the thigh releases clear juices when pricked with a fork and an instant-read thermometer inserted in the thigh registers 175°F, about 1 hour. Remove the chicken from the oven and let it rest, tented with foil, for 10 minutes. Cut the chicken into crosswise slices.

ROSEMARY-GARLIC ROAST CHICKEN

SHEILA HUNTER, CHIEF'S AIDE, BATTALION 10

Sheila—who is married to a fellow San Francisco firefighter and was a graduate of the department's first class to admit women—shares her secret for perfect roast chicken: She rubs rosemary-garlic butter under the skin, which makes the bird juicy and flavorful.

Adjust the oven rack to the center position and preheat the oven to 400°F.

Put 4 of the garlic cloves on a cutting board and coarsely chop them. Combine the rosemary and 1 teaspoon salt with the chopped garlic; continue to chop until the mixture is finely minced. In a small bowl, combine the garlic-rosemary mixture with the butter.

Starting from the top of the breast, work your fingers under the skin of one chicken, pulling it gently away from the meat, being careful not to tear the skin. Rub half of the butter mixture on the meat under the skin; you should be able to spread the mixture over the entire breast and the lower part of the thighs. Repeat with the other chicken. Season the chickens inside and out with salt and pepper; place 2 of the remaining garlic cloves in the cavity of each chicken and tie the legs together with kitchen twine.

Lightly oil a large roasting pan. Put the chickens in the pan, leaving some room between them, and put the pan in the oven. Halfway through the cooking time, baste the chickens with the pan juices and rotate them in the pan so that they cook evenly. Roast until the thighs release clear juices when pricked with a fork and an instant-read thermometer inserted in the thighs registers 175°F, about 1 hour.

Serves 6 to 8

8 cloves garlic, peeled

1 tablespoon chopped fresh rosemary

1 teaspoon salt, plus more for seasoning chicken

6 tablespoons butter, at room temperature

2 whole frying chickens (about 4 pounds each)

Freshly ground black pepper

CHICKEN GIOVACCHINI

LARRY GIOVACCHINI, CHIEF, BATTALION 36

Larry started putting this sautéed chicken and rich-tasting rice pilaf on firehouse tables back in the '70s, and he's been getting requests for it ever since. It was even featured in the 1976 charter issue of *Firehouse,* the national firefighters' magazine, which called it "a relatively inexpensive and versatile gourmet's delight," adding that "if a fire or run disturbs the firehouse at dinnertime, it can be easily resuscitated"—a handy feature for cooks faced with "putting out fires" on the home front as well.

Adjust the oven rack to the center position and preheat the oven to 350°F.

To prepare the pilaf: In a large, heavy saucepan or Dutch oven, melt the butter over medium heat. Add the onion and sauté until translucent, about 3 minutes. Stir in the chicken livers and mushrooms. Cook until the livers are lightly browned, about 3 minutes. Add the rice and stir to coat the grains evenly in the butter. Add the broth, bay leaves, and thyme. Bring to a boil while stirring; cover and place in the oven. Cook for 20 to 25 minutes, or until the broth has been absorbed. Discard the bay leaves and stir in the cheese.

While the pilaf is cooking, prepare the chicken: With a meat pounder or a heavy skillet, pound each chicken breast between sheets of waxed paper or plastic wrap to a thickness of about 1/4 inch. Mix the flour with the garlic salt, salt, and pepper on a plate. Dredge each chicken breast in the mixture, shaking off the excess.

Serves 6

CHICKEN LIVER &
MUSHROOM PILAF

3 tablespoons butter

1 medium yellow onion, diced

6 chicken livers (about 12 ounces), chopped

4 ounces mushrooms, sliced

1 1/2 cups converted long-grain rice

3 cups chicken broth

2 bay leaves

1/4 teaspoon dried thyme

1/2 cup grated Parmesan cheese

Heat half of the olive oil in a large skillet over medium-high heat and cook 3 of the chicken breasts until golden brown on each side, 3 to 4 minutes per side. Pour half of the sherry over the chicken and cook until evaporated, about 1 minute. Transfer the chicken to a plate and cover with foil to keep warm. Wipe the pan with a paper towel and repeat the process with the remaining 3 chicken breasts.

Serve the chicken breasts with the pilaf on the side and garnish each plate with chopped parsley and a lemon wedge.

6 boneless, skinless chicken breast halves (about 3 pounds total)

1 cup all-purpose flour

$1/2$ teaspoon garlic salt

$1/2$ teaspoon salt

$1/2$ teaspoon freshly ground black pepper

$1/4$ cup olive oil

$1/2$ cup dry sherry

$1/4$ cup chopped parsley for garnish

1 lemon, cut into 6 wedges, for garnish

THAI COCONUT CHICKEN

CHASE WILSON, ENGINE 32

Thai food is everywhere in San Francisco—including Station 32, where Chase likes to make this rich, tender chicken dish, which tastes a lot like *tom ka gai,* the popular Thai coconut chicken soup.

Cook the rice according to the package directions and keep warm.

Heat 3 tablespoons of the oil in a wok or large skillet over high heat. Add the onion, garlic, ginger, and chile; stir-fry until the onion is translucent, 3 to 4 minutes. Transfer the onion mixture to a bowl and set it aside.

Heat the remaining 2 tablespoons of oil in the wok and add the chicken. Stir-fry until the chicken is opaque, about 5 minutes. Return the onion mixture to the wok and add the coconut milk, soy sauce, and vinegar; bring to a gentle boil and cook over medium heat until the sauce is thickened and reduced by half, about 8 minutes. Stir in the basil, transfer the chicken and sauce to a serving bowl, and serve immediately over the rice.

Serves 4 to 6

2 cups jasmine or basmati rice

5 tablespoons vegetable oil

1 medium white onion, halved and cut into 1/4-inch slices

1 tablespoon minced garlic

2 tablespoons minced ginger

1 jalapeño chile, stemmed, halved, seeded, and thinly sliced

4 boneless, skinless chicken breast halves (about 2 pounds total), cut into 1/2-inch chunks

1 can (13 1/2) ounces coconut milk

1/4 cup soy sauce

3 tablespoons rice vinegar

1 bunch basil, leaves thinly sliced (to make about 1 cup)

TURKEY MEATLOAF

MARTY VERHAEG, ENGINE 13

"When I started in the department, dinner was definitely a meat-and-potatoes deal," says Marty. "A lot of the time it still is, but the whole thing has really lightened up a lot." His Turkey Meatloaf, made with "everything I've always put in, except the fat," is a good example. Serve it with Potatoes Fonteca (page 165).

Adjust the oven rack to the center position and preheat the oven to 350°F. Lightly grease a 9-by-13-inch baking pan.

Combine the milk and bread cubes in a small bowl and let stand for 5 minutes. In a large bowl, lightly beat the eggs. Whisk in the mustard, Worcestershire sauce, tomato paste, parsley, sage, thyme, oregano, salt, and pepper. Add the onion, turkey, sausage, and soaked bread cubes. Mix with your hands until combined; do not overmix. Gather the mixture into a ball and transfer it to the baking pan.

Using your hands, mound the mixture into a 5-by-9-inch loaf. Pour the water around the loaf. Loosely tent the pan with aluminum foil and bake the loaf for 30 minutes. Remove the foil and brush the loaf with the ketchup. Bake, uncovered, for 30 minutes more, until the loaf is cooked through. Let the loaf rest for 10 minutes before slicing.

Serves 6

½ cup low-fat milk

3 slices whole-wheat bread, cut into ¼-inch cubes

2 eggs

1 tablespoon Dijon mustard

1 tablespoon Worcestershire sauce

2 tablespoons tomato paste

½ cup chopped parsley

1 teaspoon dried sage

1 teaspoon dried thyme

1 teaspoon dried oregano

1 teaspoon salt

½ teaspoon freshly ground black pepper

1 medium yellow onion, finely diced

1 pound ground turkey

8 ounces Italian-style chicken or turkey sausage, casings removed

¼ cup water

½ cup ketchup

PACIFIC FISH TACOS

CAPT. RICH JOHNSON, ENGINE 26

"Don't let the last name fool you," says Rich. "I'm Hispanic!" No wonder his classic beer-battered fish tacos taste so good. They take a little work to prepare, but they're worth it. The trick is to do what Rich does at the firehouse: Recruit help and get all the ingredients ready ahead of time so all you have to do is fry the fish at the last minute. These are perfect served buffet style, with everything laid out on the table so people can assemble their own tacos just the way they like them. Serve "Smoke and Fire" Black Beans (page 176) on the side.

To make the Secret Sauce: Stir together the mayonnaise, vinegar, lemon juice, and sugar in a small bowl; set aside.

To make the batter: Whisk together the flour, baking powder, chili powder, salt, and pepper in a medium bowl; make a well in the center. In another bowl, beat the egg and whisk in the beer. Gradually pour the egg-beer mixture into the center of the dry ingredients, whisking until the batter is smooth. Set aside.

Cut the fish fillets into 1-by-3-inch strips. Lay the strips on paper towels to absorb any excess moisture.

Set out all the taco ingredients: the warm cooked rice, grated cheese, cabbage, salsa, avocado, and Secret Sauce.

Pour oil into a deep, heavy skillet or deep fryer to a depth of about 3 inches. Heat the oil until a candy/deep-fat thermometer registers 365°F. Fry the tortillas one at a time to soften them, using metal tongs or a slotted spatula to dip them in the hot oil for about 30 seconds each; they will remain soft, not crisp. Drain on paper towels and keep warm until ready to use.

continued on page 116

Serves 6

SECRET SAUCE
1/2 cup mayonnaise
2 tablespoons cider vinegar
2 tablespoons fresh lemon juice
1 tablespoon sugar

BEER BATTER
1 cup all-purpose flour
1/2 teaspoon baking powder
1/2 teaspoon mild chili powder
Salt and freshly ground pepper
1 egg
1 1/2 cups beer

1 1/2 pounds skinless cod or snapper fillets, pinbones removed
3 cups Mexican Red Rice (page 174)
1 cup grated Parmesan cheese
2 cups finely shredded red cabbage
1 cup Pico de Gallo Salsa (page 174)
2 avocados, pitted, peeled, and sliced crosswise 1/4 inch thick
Vegetable oil, for deep-frying
12 white corn tortillas

Frying Tips: *Use a candy/deep-fat thermometer (one that goes from 100 °F to 400 °F) to check the oil temperature, making sure the tip is immersed in the oil but is not touching the bottom of the pan. If you don't have a thermometer, check the temperature by frying a cube of white bread in the oil; it should turn golden brown after about 1 minute. You can keep the fried fish warm on a baking sheet in a 250 °F oven for up to 20 minutes.*

Working in small batches, dip the fish strips into the batter, letting the excess batter drip back into the bowl. Using tongs or a slotted spoon, carefully lower the strips into the hot oil. Fry until golden brown, about 5 minutes. Transfer to a plate lined with paper towels; keep warm. Repeat until all the fish is fried.

To assemble each taco, fill a tortilla with ¼ cup of the rice, 1 or 2 pieces of fish, some cabbage, a drizzle of Secret Sauce, 1 tablespoon of salsa, a couple of avocado slices, and a sprinkling of cheese. Serve immediately.

WHOLE ROASTED SALMON
with LEMON-BASIL TERIYAKI

MIKE CAMPANALI, TRUCK 7

From April to November, many San Francisco firefighters spend their down days out past the Golden Gate, fishing for some of the tastiest salmon in the world. They know that back at the firehouse, there's always a crowd that's eager to eat it. Roasting a whole salmon is an easy way to feed a big group, and Mike says this recipe is foolproof, as long as you remember one key ingredient: "You gotta put the love in."

To make the marinade: Combine the sherry, soy sauce, ginger, garlic, and brown sugar in a saucepan and bring to a boil. Reduce the heat to a simmer and cook for 10 minutes. Let cool to room temperature. Stir in the olive oil, lemon juice, basil, and pepper.

To marinate the fish: On a rimmed baking sheet large enough to hold the fish, spread a double layer of heavy aluminum foil, allowing 3 inches of overhang on all sides. Place the fish on the foil and roll up the foil to form a border all around the fish so that the marinade will not run onto the pan. Pour the marinade over the fish and into the belly cavity. Cover with plastic wrap and refrigerate for 45 minutes, turning the fish once.

To bake the fish: Adjust the oven rack to the center position and preheat the oven to 400°F. Sprinkle the fish with the paprika and bake, basting from time to time with the marinade, until the salmon is opaque when a knife is inserted at the center of the thickest part, about 40 minutes. Remove the skin from the salmon and use 2 spatulas to transfer it to a warm platter, leaving the head and tail intact. Garnish with the lemon wedges.

Serves 6

MARINADE

1/4 cup sherry

3/4 cup soy sauce

1 tablespoon grated fresh ginger

3 cloves garlic, minced

2 tablespoons brown sugar

1 cup olive oil

1/4 cup freshly squeezed lemon juice

Leaves from 1 large bunch basil (about 2 cups), chopped

2 teaspoons freshly ground black pepper

1 whole salmon (about 6 pounds), cleaned, head and tail left on

1 teaspoon paprika

1 lemon, cut into 6 wedges, for garnish

BAKED SALMON FILLET
with a POTATO CHIP CRUST

LT. JEANNE SEYLER, ENGINE 29

Jeanne is a third-generation San Francisco firefighter with a long family history of salmon fishing. Her dad, who is now retired, still shows up at the station every now and then with a freshly caught king salmon for Jeanne and the crew. Needless to say, he's invited to stay for dinner.

Adjust the oven rack to the center position and preheat the oven to 375°F.

In a small bowl, combine the crushed potato chips, bread crumbs, dill, and garlic; set aside.

Put the salmon skin-side down on a lightly oiled, foil-lined rimmed baking sheet. Remove any pinbones with a pair of needle-nose pliers. Brush the surface of the salmon with the mustard, spreading it evenly. Sprinkle the potato chip mixture over the mustard, packing it lightly with your fingertips so that it adheres to the surface. Season with the pepper.

Bake until the crust is golden brown and the salmon is opaque when a knife is inserted at the center of the thickest part, about 30 minutes. Using 2 spatulas, carefully transfer the fillet in one piece to a large serving platter, leaving the skin on the baking sheet; garnish with the lemon wedges and dill sprigs.

Serves 6

1/2 cup crushed potato chips

1/4 cup bread crumbs

1 teaspoon dried dill

1 clove garlic, pressed

1 large salmon fillet (about 3 pounds), skin on

2 tablespoons Dijon mustard

Freshly ground black pepper

GARNISHES

1 lemon, cut into 6 wedges

Fresh dill sprigs

FIREHOUSE 11 CIOPPINO

DARRYL DAIR, TRUCK 11

Cioppino, a rich tomato and seafood stew, is said to have been invented in San Francisco by Italian immigrants. At Station 11 in Noe Valley, Darryl adds his own spin, serving his intense, brothy version over linguine. At home, he makes it with both red and white wine, but he says chicken broth is a great substitute when he serves it at the firehouse.

Put the garlic, celery, onion, and carrots in a food processor and process until finely chopped. In a large, heavy-bottomed soup pot or Dutch oven with a tight-fitting lid, heat the oil over medium heat; add the chopped vegetables and sauté for 5 minutes. Add the red wine and cook for 5 minutes more. Stir in the tomatoes, chiles, bay leaves, parsley, and sugar. Bring to a boil, reduce the heat to low, and simmer for 45 minutes. Add the white wine, oregano, thyme, and basil. Return to a simmer and continue to cook for 30 minutes.

Stir in the prawns, fish, and crab; simmer until they are cooked through, 5 to 10 minutes.

Meanwhile, cook the linguine in boiling salted water according to the package directions; drain and keep warm for serving.

Layer the clams on top of the cioppino, discarding any that are broken or are open and do not close when touched. Cover and cook over medium heat until the clams are steamed open, about 5 minutes. Discard any clams that have not opened. Discard the chiles and bay leaves. Season to taste with salt and pepper.

Divide the linguine among 6 soup bowls and ladle the cioppino over the noodles, distributing the seafood evenly among the bowls.

Serves 6

5 cloves garlic, peeled

2 stalks celery, coarsely chopped

1 large yellow onion, coarsely chopped

2 carrots, peeled and coarsely chopped

1/4 cup olive oil

1 cup red wine or chicken broth

2 cans (28 ounces each) crushed tomatoes in purée

1 or 2 jalapeño chiles, slit along one side

2 bay leaves

1/2 cup chopped Italian parsley

1 tablespoon sugar

1 cup white wine or chicken broth

1/2 teaspoon dried oregano

1/2 teaspoon dried thyme

1/2 teaspoon dried basil

2 pounds medium prawns, peeled and deveined

1 pound fish fillets, such as snapper or sea bass, cut into 2-inch pieces

3 or 4 cooked Dungeness crabs, cleaned and quartered (see page 83)

1 pound dried linguine

2 pounds Manila or littleneck clams, scrubbed

Salt and freshly ground black pepper

STUFFED SOLE FILLETS

RICHARD V. STARK, ENGINE 34

Richard has a thing about the Pacific. He grew up in San Francisco, four blocks from the ocean, and ended up working at Station 34, just up the road from the coast. His stuffed sole makes a great impression at the table, and it's not hard to prepare. "I learned how to cook by hanging around in the firehouse kitchen and watching the old-timers, studying their tricks," he says. "Now, 25 years later, I'm the old-timer. Funny how that works."

To make the filling: Squeeze the excess water from the spinach, using your hands. Melt the butter in a large, heavy skillet over medium heat and sauté the shallots until tender, about 3 minutes. Add the mushrooms and sauté until lightly browned, about 5 minutes. Remove from the heat and stir in the shrimp, spinach, almonds, and fresh herbs. Season to taste with salt and pepper. Allow the mixture to cool.

Adjust the oven rack to the center position and preheat the oven to 400°F. Lightly butter a 9-by-13-inch baking pan.

Place the sole fillets on a flat work surface with the wider ends facing you. Season with salt and pepper. Spread the filling on the fillets, leaving a 1-inch border at the far end of each. Starting with the end nearest you, roll up a fillet, enclosing the filling, and secure the end with a toothpick. Repeat with the remaining fillets. Place the rolled fillets in the baking pan and pour the wine, lemon juice, and olive oil over them. Scatter the cherry tomato halves and chopped parsley over all. Bake, basting occasionally with the pan juices, until the fish is cooked through, about 20 minutes.

To serve, place the rolls on individual plates and remove the toothpicks. Spoon the tomatoes and some of the pan juices over the fish. Garnish each with the almonds, a sprig of parsley, and a lemon wedge.

Serves 6

FILLING

1 package (10 ounces) frozen chopped spinach, thawed

4 tablespoons (½ stick) butter

4 shallots, minced

8 ounces mushrooms, finely chopped

8 ounces bay shrimp, chopped

⅓ cup sliced almonds, toasted (see page 163), plus extra for garnish

2 tablespoons chopped mixed fresh herbs (such as rosemary, oregano, basil, and thyme)

Salt and freshly ground pepper

6 skinless sole fillets (6 to 8 ounces each)

Salt and freshly ground pepper

2 cups dry white wine

Juice of 1 lemon (2 to 3 tablespoons)

2 tablespoons extra-virgin olive oil

1 pint cherry tomatoes; halved

¼ cup chopped Italian parsley

Italian parsley sprigs for garnish

1 lemon, cut into 6 wedges, for garnish

GREEN CURRY SALMON

RICH WAGNER, ENGINE 10

In a city with Asian markets in nearly every neighborhood, it's not unusual to find ingredients like Thai green curry paste, fish sauce, and coconut milk in the pantry of a firehouse kitchen. Keep them on hand in *your* house, and you can throw together a quick, authentic-tasting curry like this one on short notice. This recipe works well with any firm-fleshed fish, as well as medium prawns (peeled and deveined) or tofu.

Cook the rice according to the package directions and keep warm.

While the rice is cooking, heat the oil in a wok or large, deep-sided skillet over medium-high heat. Add the ginger and curry paste and cook, stirring, for 2 minutes. Add the bell pepper, coconut milk, broth, fish sauce, lime juice, and sugar; bring to a boil and cook until reduced by half. Add the salmon, green onions, mushrooms, and bamboo shoots. Bring to a boil, then reduce the heat to low and simmer until the salmon is just cooked through, about 5 minutes.

Transfer to a serving bowl and garnish with the cilantro. Serve with the rice.

Serves 6

2 cups jasmine or basmati rice

1 tablespoon vegetable oil

1 tablespoon minced fresh ginger

1 tablespoon Thai-style green curry paste (such as Thai Kitchen brand)

1/2 medium red bell pepper, stemmed, seeded, and cut into 1/4-inch strips

1 can (14 ounces) unsweetened coconut milk

1/2 cup chicken broth

3 tablespoons Thai or Vietnamese fish sauce

1 tablespoon freshly squeezed lime juice

2 teaspoons sugar

2 pounds filleted salmon, skin removed, cut into 1-inch cubes

6 green onions, white and pale green parts only, thinly sliced on the diagonal

1 can (15 ounces) Asian straw mushrooms, drained, or 6 ounces fresh button mushrooms, sliced

1 can (8 ounces) sliced bamboo shoots, drained

Cilantro sprigs for garnish

122 | FIREHOUSE FOOD

KUNG PAO PRAWNS

MICHAEL CARION, ENGINE 14

"I can't cook at home," says Michael with a chuckle. "My wife won't let me." That's because she comes from a family of Chinese restaurant owners, and her kitchen is her castle. So Michael gets his culinary kicks at the firehouse, where he likes to introduce the crew to the kinds of Chinese specialties he learned when he was growing up, like these succulent, fiery prawns. If you're not partial to spicy food, just reduce the amount of chiles and chili oil.

Cook the rice according to the package directions and keep warm.

Heat the vegetable oil over high heat in a wok or large, deep-sided skillet. Add the prawns, garlic, and chiles; stir-fry for 2 minutes. Stir in the chili oil, soy sauce, sugar, and vinegar. Add the peanuts, carrot, and celery. Stir to combine and reduce the heat to low. Cover and cook for 3 minutes.

Meanwhile, whisk together the broth and cornstarch in a small bowl. Add the cornstarch mixture to the wok, stir to combine, and bring to a boil. Cook until the sauce thickens, 2 to 3 minutes. Stir in the sesame oil and season to taste with salt.

Garnish with the green onions and serve with the rice.

Serves 4 to 6

2 cups long-grain white rice

1 tablespoon vegetable oil

2 pounds medium prawns, peeled and deveined

2 cloves garlic, minced

3 small dried red chiles, such as arbol

1 to 2 teaspoons chili oil

2 tablespoons soy sauce

1/2 teaspoon sugar

1 teaspoon distilled white vinegar

1/2 cup dry-roasted peanuts

1 medium carrot, peeled and thinly sliced on the diagonal

1 stalk celery, thinly sliced on the diagonal

1/2 cup chicken broth

1 teaspoon cornstarch

2 teaspoons Asian sesame oil

Salt

3 green onions, white and pale green parts only, thinly sliced on the diagonal, for garnish

BLACKENED RED SNAPPER

BARRY COMERFORD, ENGINE 7

Barry credits Lt. Ed Bryant (retired) with the original version of this New Orleans–style recipe, but he has added a few adaptations of his own. Blackened fish is usually more of a restaurant dish than one to enjoy at home, because searing it in a hot iron skillet produces lots of pungent smoke. This version, though, is made on the grill, so there's no need to worry about setting off your smoke alarm—or having to call the fire department. The Blackening Rub can also be used on chicken, beef, or pork. Barry suggests serving this with a rice pilaf.

To make the rub: Combine the white and black pepper, cayenne, onion salt, garlic powder, paprika, thyme, and salt in a small bowl.

To prepare the fish: Rinse the fish fillets and dry them well with paper towels. Remove any pinbones with a pair of needle-nose pliers or tweezers. Coat both sides of the fish generously with the rub and refrigerate for 1 hour.

Prepare the grill with a medium-hot fire (see page 99). Drizzle the butter on both sides of the fillets. Grill the fish until the rub is lightly charred and the fish is cooked through but still moist, 2 to 3 minutes per side. Serve with the lemon wedges and tartar sauce.

Serves 6

BLACKENING RUB

1 teaspoon ground white pepper

1 teaspoon freshly ground black pepper

1/4 teaspoon cayenne pepper

1 teaspoon onion salt

1 teaspoon garlic powder

2 teaspoons paprika

1 teaspoon dried thyme

1 teaspoon salt

6 skinless red snapper fillets (8 ounces each)

4 tablespoons (1/2 stick) butter, melted

ACCOMPANIMENTS

1 lemon, cut into 6wedges

Ed's Tartar Sauce (page 103)

DUNGENESS CRAB CAKES

DARRYL DAIR, TRUCK 11

Crab is big at Station 11, especially between November and June. That's when the "lobster of the West," Dungeness crab, is in season, and many of the members go crabbing together on their days off, then bring their catch back to the house for everyone to enjoy. Darryl's crab cakes are a favorite at the station, and, he points out, they're even a hit with his toughest critic: his son. Serve them with a green salad and some sourdough French bread.

Mix the crabmeat with the mayonnaise, mustard, green onions, and ⅓ cup of the bread crumbs in a large bowl. Season the mixture to taste with salt and pepper. Form the mixture into 12 flat cakes, about ½ inch thick and 2 to 3 inches in diameter.

Spread the remaining ⅔ cup bread crumbs on a plate and coat the crab cakes on both sides and on their edges with the crumbs. Refrigerate the cakes for at least 30 minutes.

Heat 2 tablespoons of the olive oil and 2 tablespoons of the butter in a large skillet over medium-high heat. Put 6 crab cakes in the pan and fry until golden brown and heated through, about 3 minutes on each side. Transfer the cakes to a plate lined with a paper towel and keep warm. Discard any oil remaining in the pan and wipe out the inside with a paper towel. Heat the remaining 2 tablespoons oil and 2 tablespoons butter in the pan and fry the remaining 6 crab cakes in the same way. Serve warm with the lemon wedges and tartar sauce on the side.

Serves 6

1 pound cooked Dungeness crabmeat (see page 83), picked over for shell fragments

½ cup mayonnaise

2 tablespoons Dijon mustard

3 green onions, white and pale green parts only, finely chopped

1 cup Italian-style bread crumbs

Salt and freshly ground black pepper

¼ cup olive oil

4 tablespoons (½ stick) butter

ACCOMPANIMENTS

1 lemon, cut into 6 wedges

Ed's Tartar Sauce (page 103)

GRANDMA MILICI'S SPAGHETTI and MEATBALLS

ROBERT MILICI, ENGINE 9

Calling all carnivores: You've found the pasta of your dreams. The sauce is made with slow-simmered pork ribs and hot Italian sausage in the traditional southern Italian way, and the meatballs combine beef, veal, and pork for exceptional flavor and texture. The recipe "definitely serves a double house," says Bob, "which would be 10 firefighters . . . or 12 normal people." Have a crowd over and serve this with garlic bread and a big Firehouse Caesar Salad (page 46). Or skip the crowd and make the whole batch of sauce anyway—the leftovers freeze beautifully.

To make the sauce: Heat the olive oil in the bottom of a large, heavy-bottomed soup pot or Dutch oven over medium-high heat. Add the onion and salt, reduce the heat to medium, and cover the pot. Cook for 2 to 3 minutes, until the onion is wilted and translucent, stirring occasionally. Add the garlic, basil, oregano, and Italian seasoning; cook, uncovered, for 2 more minutes. Add the tomatoes, tomato purée, tomato paste, and water. (A quick way to measure the water is to fill one of the 28-ounce cans twice.) Stir in the sugar and add the whole sausages and pork ribs to the sauce. Bring the sauce to a boil, then reduce the heat to low. Simmer the sauce, uncovered, while you prepare the meatballs.

To make the meatballs: Beat the eggs with the milk in a small bowl and set aside. In a large bowl, combine the ground beef, veal, and pork and gently mix them with your hands. Avoid kneading and overmixing: The lighter the touch you use, the less dense the meatballs will be. Sprinkle the garlic, parsley, cheese, ½ cup of the bread crumbs, salt, and pepper evenly over the meat. Pour in the egg mixture and use your hands to combine all the ingredients. The mixture should be firm and easy to work with. If it is too soft, add more bread crumbs.

Serves 12

SAUCE

¼ cup olive oil

1 medium yellow onion, chopped

1 tablespoon salt

2 tablespoons minced garlic

3 tablespoons minced fresh basil or 1 tablespoon dried basil

3 tablespoons minced fresh oregano or 1 tablespoon dried oregano

2 teaspoons dried Italian seasoning

1 can (28 ounces) crushed tomatoes

1 can (28 ounces) tomato purée

1 can (12 ounces) tomato paste

7 cups water

1 tablespoon sugar

1 pound hot Italian sausages

1 pound bone-in country-style pork ribs (or pork spareribs), cut into individual pieces

"My grandfather, Pompeo Scipio Milici, was 100 percent Sicilian. When he married my grandmother, Peggy, who was Czech and not too experienced in the kitchen, Pompeo's mother did what she had to do—she taught Grandma Peggy how to cook for her 'baby.' Spaghetti and meatballs was a Sunday-night tradition in my great-grandmother's home, so that was the first dish she taught Grandma. Pompeo had a bit of a temper, and a lot of plates of spaghetti ended up on the wall before Grandma finally got the recipe right."

Roll 36 golf ball–sized meatballs, making them as round and free of cracks as possible. Gently place the meatballs in the sauce. You should have enough liquid to cover the meatballs completely; if not, add some water. Let the sauce simmer without stirring for 30 minutes; this will allow the meatballs to firm up. Continue to simmer, stirring occasionally, until the rib meat is very tender and falling away from the bones, about 3 hours.

Using a slotted spoon, transfer the meatballs to a bowl; remove the sausages and ribs from the sauce and put them on a cutting board. When they have cooled slightly, slice the sausages into rounds; use a fork to pull the rib meat away from the bones and shred it, discarding the bones and any large pieces of fat. Skim off and discard any fat that has risen to the top of the sauce. Stir the sausage slices, rib meat, and meatballs into the sauce and season, if needed, with salt and pepper.

Cook the spaghetti in boiling salted water according to the package directions. Drain and toss with most of the sauce in a large bowl. Top each serving of spaghetti with a little additional sauce and 3 meatballs. Garnish with Parmesan and chopped parsley.

MEATBALLS

3 eggs

1/2 cup milk

2 pounds ground beef

1 pound ground veal

1 pound ground pork

2 tablespoons finely minced garlic

1/2 cup chopped Italian parsley

1/2 cup grated Parmesan cheese

1/2 to 3/4 cup bread crumbs

1 tablespoon salt

2 teaspoons freshly ground black pepper

2 to 2 1/2 pounds dried spaghetti

GARNISHES

Grated Parmesan cheese

Chopped parsley

PASTA PUTTANESCA

ALISON YEE, ENGINE 12

This recipe, which Alison describes as "very popular, very easy, reasonably healthy, and pretty quick," was passed on to her by a fellow firefighter, and she has since adapted it a bit to suit her own taste. It's a good choice for a warm summer evening. If you're cooking for vegetarians, just leave out the anchovies.

Heat the olive oil in a large skillet or Dutch oven over medium heat and sauté the garlic until tender, about 2 minutes. Crush the tomatoes with your hands and add them, with their liquid, to the skillet. Stir in the olives, capers, red pepper flakes, and oregano. Bring to a boil and reduce the heat to low. Simmer for 30 minutes, stirring from time to time.

Once the sauce has simmered for about 20 minutes, cook the pasta in boiling salted water according to the package directions. Drain the pasta and put it in a large serving bowl.

When ready to serve, stir the anchovies and parsley into the sauce and cook for 1 minute. Season to taste with pepper. Pour the sauce over the pasta, toss to combine, and serve immediately. Pass the grated cheese at the table.

Serves 6 as a first course or 4 as a main course

¼ cup extra-virgin olive oil

5 cloves garlic, chopped

1 can (28 ounces) whole plum tomatoes

1 cup mixed olives, pitted and diced

4 teaspoons drained capers, chopped

½ teaspoon red pepper flakes

½ teaspoon dried oregano

1 pound dried long pasta, such as spaghetti, linguine, or bucatini

1 can (2 ounces) anchovy fillets, drained and chopped

¼ cup chopped Italian parsley

Freshly ground black pepper

Grated Asiago or Parmesan cheese for serving

C-WATCH FRIED MEIN
with OYSTER SAUCE BEEF JOHN CHUNG AND NORM KWAN, ENGINE 17

With a ready supply of fresh noodles from the H&E Chinese Noodle Factory down the block from the firehouse, John and Norm are never at a loss for lunch or dinner ideas. Their easy noodle-frying technique produces a wonderful contrast of chewy and crispy textures, and noodles made in this way can be topped with just about anything. John and Norm tend to cook without recipes, using whatever's fresh and on special at the local grocery store. If steak's looking pricey, they'll often make this dish with ground beef.

Coat the flank steak with 3 tablespoons of the soy sauce in a shallow dish and marinate for 30 minutes, turning once. Cut the meat across the grain into very thin slices.

Prepare an ice bath by filling a large bowl with water and ice. Bring a large pot of lightly salted water to a boil. Add the snap peas and cook until crisp-tender, about 1 minute. Remove the peas from the water with a slotted spoon, reserving the boiling water, and transfer to the ice bath to cool. Drain and set aside.

Cook the noodles in the boiling water for 1 minute less than directed on the package, or until they are al dente; they will be cooked more when fried. Drain in a colander and rinse under cold water. Drain well and transfer to a bowl. Toss the noodles in the sesame oil and the remaining 3 tablespoons soy sauce. Set aside until ready to fry.

Heat 3 tablespoons of the peanut oil in a large nonstick skillet over medium heat. Add the noodles and flatten them into a pancake using the back of a spatula. Cook without stirring for 5 minutes, until lightly browned. Flip over and cook the other side in the same way. Transfer to a plate and keep warm.

Serves 6

1½ pounds flank steak

6 tablespoons soy sauce

12 ounces sugar snap peas

1 pound fresh Chinese egg noodles

1 tablespoon Asian sesame oil

5 tablespoons peanut oil

½ cup water

1 yellow onion, thinly sliced

2 tablespoons Asian oyster sauce

1 teaspoon cornstarch dissolved in
  ¼ cup chicken broth

6 green onions, white and pale green
  parts only, thinly sliced on the
  diagonal, for garnish

When John's cooking at Station 17 in Hunter's Point, he'll often pick up some noodles from his friend Hing at the nearby H&E Chinese Noodle Factory. Money rarely changes hands, and John always leaves with a little something extra—a case of fortune cookies or whatever Hing can slip under his arm.

Heat 1 tablespoon of the peanut oil in the skillet over high heat; add the snap peas and stir-fry for 2 minutes. Add the water; cover and steam for 1 minute. Transfer to a plate with a slotted spoon.

Wipe out the skillet with a paper towel. Heat the remaining tablespoon of peanut oil in the skillet over medium heat. Add the yellow onion and stir-fry for 4 minutes, until soft and golden. Add the meat to the skillet and stir-fry for 5 minutes. Add the oyster sauce and the cornstarch mixture. Stir to combine and cook for 1 to 2 minutes longer, until the sauce is thickened to the consistency of gravy.

Divide the noodles into 6 portions and top each with some of the sugar snap peas and beef; garnish with the green onions.

RIGATONI ALLA CARBONARA
CLAUDIO RIVIECCIO, ENGINE 40

Carbonara is traditionally made with eggs, pancetta (Italian bacon), cheese, and plenty of pepper. The hot pasta cooks the eggs on contact, forming a rich, golden sauce. In Claudio's family, the sauce also includes cream. Claudio grew up in North Beach and is fluent in Italian—especially when it comes to cooking. "My mom's from Genova, and my dad grew up working in his family's pizzeria in Naples, so I've eaten great Italian food my whole life," he says. "In fact, I have absolutely no idea how to make anything else!" So far, no one at Station 40 has objected.

Cook the pancetta in a large, heavy skillet over medium-low heat until it is browned, about 5 minutes. Remove the pancetta, using a slotted spoon; drain on paper towels and set aside.

Discard all but 1 tablespoon of the rendered fat in the skillet. Add the oil and heat the skillet briefly over medium heat; add the mushrooms and red pepper flakes and sauté until the mushrooms are golden, 4 to 5 minutes. Add the cream and increase the heat to medium-high. Cook until the cream has thickened slightly, about 4 minutes. Keep warm.

In a bowl large enough to hold the pasta, beat the eggs and yolk with the cheese. Cook the rigatoni in boiling salted water according to the package directions. Reserve 1/2 cup of the pasta water and drain the rigatoni in a colander.

Immediately add the hot pasta to the bowl with the egg mixture, stirring to combine. Stir in the warm mushroom mixture, pancetta, parsley, and pepper. If the pasta seems dry or the sauce too thick, add a few tablespoons of the reserved pasta water. Serve immediately in large, shallow bowls. Pass additional grated cheese at the table.

Serves 6 as a first course or 4 as a main course

8 ounces thick-cut pancetta or bacon, sliced crosswise into 1/4-inch strips

1 tablespoon olive oil

8 ounces mushrooms, sliced

Dash of red pepper flakes

1 cup whipping cream

2 eggs

1 egg yolk

1 cup grated Pecorino Romano or Parmesan cheese, plus extra for serving

1 pound dried rigatoni

2 tablespoons chopped Italian parsley

1 teaspoon freshly ground black pepper

POLENTA LASAGNA

KAREN KERR, ENGINE 7

"When I started out as a firefighter, I didn't really get how important the meals were," says Karen. "But pretty soon, I realized how lucky I am that I like to cook—and how much fun cooking can be in a big kitchen with great equipment, lots of people to help with the prep, an appreciative audience, and best of all, a whole crew insisting on doing the dishes afterwards." She learned how to make this dish from firefighter Albert Jones at Station 10, right after her first year of probationary training. She's since adapted it to her own style of cooking, and it has become her signature firehouse dish. Like most lasagnas, it takes a bit of work, because you have to prepare all the components in advance. But, like most lasagnas, it's worth it. Serve it with a green salad and Karen's other signature: homemade Tuscan Rolls (page 178).

To make the marinara sauce: Heat the olive oil in a large, heavy-bottomed pot or Dutch oven over medium heat. Add the onion and sauté until translucent. Add the ground turkey, if using, and cook, breaking up any large pieces of meat, until lightly browned, about 8 minutes. Add the tomatoes, tomato paste, and bay leaves. Season to taste with salt and pepper. Bring to a boil, reduce the heat to low, and simmer for 45 minutes. Just before assembling the lasagna, discard the bay leaves and stir in the parsley, thyme, and vinegar. (Makes about 5 cups of sauce.)

Meanwhile, prepare the polenta as directed. Cover a large, flat surface (about 16 by 30 inches) with plastic wrap or parchment paper. Pour the cooked polenta onto the plastic wrap, spreading it out evenly with a rubber spatula into a rectangle, about 12 by 24 inches and about 1/4 inch thick. Allow it to cool, then cut it into eighteen 4-inch squares.

continued on page 138

Serves 6 to 8

MARINARA SAUCE

2 tablespoons olive oil

1 large yellow onion, diced

1 pound lean ground turkey (optional)

3 cans (28 ounces each) diced tomatoes

1 can (12 ounces) tomato paste

2 bay leaves

Salt and freshly ground black pepper

3 tablespoons chopped Italian parsley

1 tablespoon chopped fresh thyme leaves

1 tablespoon balsamic vinegar

Creamy Polenta (page 172)

Along with seven women firefighters, Karen cofounded Camp Blaze, a weeklong leadership camp for young women, aged 16 to 19, that gives them a taste of firefighting. "We do live-fire training, search and rescue techniques, team-building skills . . . everything but cooking!" says Karen. "Some will become firefighters, some won't. But by the end of the week, they're all charged. They can do anything."

POLENTA LASAGNA *continued*

To make the béchamel sauce: Heat the butter in a small saucepan over low heat. Sprinkle in the flour and stir to form a thick paste. Cook for 1 minute, stirring; do not allow the mixture to brown. Whisk in the milk and cook until the sauce has thickened and coats the back of a wooden spoon, about 10 minutes. Season with the nutmeg, paprika, salt, and pepper. Set aside.

To prepare the vegetables: Heat the olive oil in a large skillet over medium heat. Add the garlic and sauté for 1 minute. Add the carrots and bell peppers and sauté for 3 minutes more. Stir in the zucchini and sauté for 1 minute. Add the mushrooms and sauté for 2 minutes. Season to taste with salt and pepper. Set aside.

Preheat the oven to 350°F.

To assemble the lasagna: Lightly oil a deep-sided 9-by-13-inch baking pan. Spread 1 cup marinara sauce over the bottom of the pan. Line the bottom of the pan with a layer of 6 polenta squares. Spread 1⅓ cups marinara sauce over the polenta, followed by half of the sautéed vegetables, one third of the mozzarella, one third of the Parmesan, and half of the béchamel. Repeat the process with an identical layer of 6 polenta squares, 1⅓ cups marinara sauce, the remaining vegetables, one third of the mozzarella, one third of the Parmesan, and the remaining béchamel. Finish with a third layer of polenta squares topped with 1⅓ cups marinara sauce and the remaining mozzarella and Parmesan. Cover with aluminum foil and bake for 45 minutes to an hour. Let stand for 15 minutes before serving.

BÉCHAMEL SAUCE

2 tablespoons butter

1½ tablespoons all-purpose flour

1¾ cups whole milk

Pinch of ground nutmeg

Pinch of paprika

Salt and freshly ground black pepper

¼ cup olive oil

8 cloves garlic, minced

2 large carrots, peeled and diced

2 medium yellow bell peppers, stemmed, seeded, and diced

3 to 4 medium zucchini, diced

8 ounces mushrooms, sliced

Salt and freshly ground black pepper

1 pound mozzarella or Jack cheese, grated

1 cup grated Parmesan cheese

PENNE with CHICKEN and ARTICHOKES

TRACE McCULLOCH, ENGINE 21

When you want to feed a lot of people without blowing your budget, a big bowl of pasta can be just the thing. Like many firehouse recipes, this one is flexible and forgiving: You can substitute prawns for the chicken, or use a combination of vegetables—like zucchini, yellow squash, mushrooms, and bell peppers—and you've got a terrific vegetarian entrée.

Cook the pasta in boiling salted water according to the package directions.

While the pasta is cooking, heat the olive oil in a large skillet over medium-high heat; add the garlic and chicken cubes. Sauté until the chicken is cooked through and lightly browned, about 5 minutes. Using a slotted spoon, transfer the chicken to a bowl and set aside. Pour the wine into the skillet and allow it to boil briefly, while scraping the brown bits from the bottom with a wooden spoon. Add the artichokes, dried tomatoes, green onions, and lemon zest. Cook over medium heat for 3 minutes, stirring gently from time to time. Return the chicken to the skillet, add the cheese, and stir to combine. Season to taste with salt and pepper.

Transfer the sauce to a large serving bowl; add the drained cooked pasta and the basil and toss to combine well. Serve immediately in large, shallow bowls. Pass additional grated cheese at the table.

Serves 6

1 pound dried penne

3 tablespoons olive oil

1 tablespoon chopped garlic

4 boneless, skinless chicken breast halves (about 1½ pounds total), cut into ½ -inch cubes

1 cup dry white wine or chicken broth

2 cans (14 ounces each) quartered artichoke hearts, drained

1 cup julienned sun-dried tomatoes in oil

1 bunch green onions, white and pale green parts only, chopped

1 tablespoon grated lemon zest (from 1 medium lemon)

1 cup grated Parmesan or Asiago cheese, plus extra for serving

Salt and freshly ground black pepper

½ cup fresh basil leaves, cut into thin strips

POLENTA with SAUSAGE and ROASTED PEPPERS

JASON HARRELL, ENGINE 39

Jason's friends Jen and Alvin passed this recipe along to him, because they thought it would be ideal for a firehouse meal—flavorful, hearty, easy to make, and economical. Try it at home for all the same reasons.

Bring the broth to a boil in a large, heavy pot; reduce the heat to medium-low. Slowly pour in the cornmeal, stirring constantly with a whisk to prevent lumps from forming. Reduce the heat to low and simmer, stirring frequently with a wooden spoon, until smooth and creamy, about 20 minutes.

Meanwhile, in a heavy skillet, heat the olive oil over medium heat. Add the sausage and break it up into small pieces with a wooden spoon. Sauté until lightly browned and cooked through, about 8 minutes. Remove from the heat.

When the cornmeal is cooked, add the sausage to it, using a slotted spoon in order to leave as much fat in the skillet as possible. To the cornmeal, add the parsley, Cheddar, mozzarella, Parmesan, bell peppers, and pesto. Season to taste with salt and pepper. Serve warm in shallow bowls.

Serves 6

6 cups chicken or vegetable broth

1 1/2 cups yellow cornmeal

2 tablespoons olive oil

12 ounces sweet Italian sausage, casings removed

1/4 cup chopped Italian parsley

1/4 cup grated Cheddar cheese

1/4 cup grated mozzarella cheese

1/4 cup grated Parmesan cheese

1 jar (7 1/4 ounces) roasted red bell peppers, diced, or 2 red bell peppers, roasted (see facing page), stemmed, seeded, and diced

1/2 cup (4 ounces) prepared pesto

Salt and freshly ground black pepper

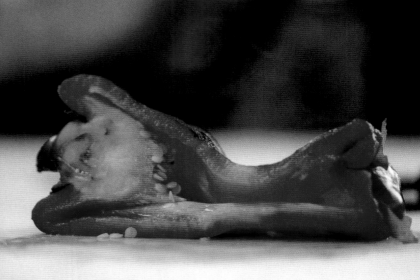

Roasting Peppers: *Use this method to roast bell peppers or fresh chiles, such as poblanos or jalapeños. If you need only a few peppers, roast them one at a time over a gas burner, holding them with tongs a few inches above the flame and turning them so that they char evenly. If you don't have a gas stove, or need to roast several peppers at a time, coat them lightly with vegetable oil and roast them under the broiler on a foil-lined, rimmed baking sheet, turning them occasionally, until they are evenly charred. Roast bell peppers until they are well blackened, chiles just until they are lightly charred and blistered. Put the just-roasted peppers in a heavy plastic bag, seal the bag, and let the peppers sit for 15 minutes so that the steam they release softens their skins. Remove them from the bag, being careful to save any juices that have collected, and scrape away the charred skins with a paring knife.*

RISOTTO with PRAWNS

CLIFF MERRILL, ENGINE 28

Cliff's wife, Elaine, gave him this recipe, thinking it might be something the crew at Station 28 would enjoy. She was right. Making good risotto isn't hard to do; it just takes a little patience. Add the hot broth to the rice in small amounts, stirring constantly, and don't add more until you can see the bottom of the pan when you drag the spoon through the rice. Plan on about 20 minutes of cooking time in all. This recipe can also be made with bay scallops, crabmeat, or, if you feel like a splurge, lobster.

Bring the broth to a steady simmer in a large saucepan.

Meanwhile, heat the olive oil in a large skillet or Dutch oven over medium heat. Add the onion and sauté until it is translucent and wilted, 3 to 4 minutes. Add the rice, stirring to coat the grains with oil. Continue cooking, stirring frequently, until the rice is translucent, about 4 minutes. Pour in the wine and cook, stirring, until the liquid is completely absorbed by the rice, 2 to 3 minutes. Stir in the diced tomatoes and saffron threads.

Start adding the hot broth in $1/2$-cup increments, stirring continuously, until each addition of broth has been absorbed. Stir in the prawns and peas along with the last addition of broth. Cook until the prawns are cooked through, the liquid has been absorbed, and the rice is creamy and slightly al dente. Stir the butter into the risotto; season to taste with salt and pepper. Spoon into warmed pasta bowls and garnish each serving with some chopped parsley.

Serves 6

5 cups chicken broth

3 tablespoons extra-virgin olive oil

1 small yellow onion, chopped

$1^1/2$ cups medium-grain rice, preferably Arborio

$1/2$ cup white wine

1 can ($14^1/2$ ounces) diced Italian-style tomatoes, drained

$1/2$ teaspoon saffron threads

1 pound medium prawns, peeled and deveined

$1/2$ cup frozen peas

2 tablespoons butter, at room temperature

Salt and freshly ground black pepper

2 tablespoons chopped parsley for garnish

ARTICHOKE and MUSHROOM FOCACCIA

LT. RICHARD BUSALACCHI, TRUCK 19

Store-bought frozen bread dough makes a perfect soft crust for this substantial meatless pizza bread. To make an even easier treat, top the same dough with Marinara Sauce (page 136) and chopped green onions.

Lightly oil the bottom and sides of a 9-by-13-inch pan.

Warm 1 tablespoon of the oil in a wide skillet over medium heat and sauté the onion until tender, about 5 minutes. Stir in the sugar and continue to cook until golden, about 3 minutes. Transfer to a bowl.

Heat another tablespoon of oil in the skillet and sauté the artichoke hearts until lightly browned, about 4 minutes. Put them in the bowl with the onion. Increase the heat to medium-high and add another tablespoon of olive oil. Toss in the mushroom slices and sauté them until browned, about 3 minutes. Add the mushrooms to the bowl with the onion and artichokes.

To assemble the focaccia, place the dough in the baking dish and stretch it out to fit the pan size, using your hands. Turn the dough over and stretch it to the edges of the pan again. Combine the Parmesan and Jack cheeses with the onion, artichokes, and mushrooms. Spread the mixture over the dough, pressing it slightly into the surface. Sprinkle with the salt and rosemary, if using. Let rest for 1 hour in a warm place.

Adjust the oven rack to the center position and preheat the oven to 450°F. Drizzle the focaccia with a little olive oil and bake for 20 minutes, until the bread is puffed and cooked through and the topping is lightly browned. Cut into squares with a serrated knife and serve warm or at room temperature.

Serves 6

3 tablespoons extra-virgin olive oil, plus more for drizzling

1 large yellow onion, sliced

1 teaspoon sugar

1 can (14 ounces) quartered artichoke hearts, drained

8 ounces mushrooms, sliced

1/2 cup grated Parmesan cheese

1/2 cup diced Jack cheese

1 loaf (1 pound) frozen bread dough (such as Bridgeford's brand), thawed according to package directions

1/2 teaspoon coarse salt

1 tablespoon chopped fresh rosemary (optional)

JOE'S SPECIAL

This spinach-and-beef scramble is a San Francisco original and a part of the culinary legacy of the city's firehouses. So who is Joe? Most people associate this dish with the venerable Joe's Italian restaurants around the Bay, where you can still find it on the menu. But some say it was invented as a luxury meal during the gold rush, when eggs sold for a dollar apiece. And others will tell you it was created by local jazz musicians in the '20s as a midnight snack. Wherever it came from, every San Francisco firefighter seems to know how to make it, and this recipe is a combination of several current versions. Serve it for brunch, dinner, or at midnight with thick-cut sourdough toast and hot sauce on the side.

Heat 1 tablespoon of the oil in a large skillet over medium-high heat. Add the beef and cook, stirring to break up the meat, until it is evenly browned, about 10 minutes. Using a slotted spoon, transfer the meat to a large bowl, draining and discarding the fat.

Return the pan to the heat and add another tablespoon of oil. Add the onion and garlic and sauté until golden and translucent, about 4 minutes. Transfer to the bowl with the beef, leaving as much oil in the pan as possible. Add the mushrooms to the pan, along with the remaining tablespoon of oil, if needed. Cook, stirring occasionally, until the mushrooms are lightly browned, about 5 minutes.

Return the beef and onion to the pan with the mushrooms. Add the spinach, Worcestershire sauce, Italian seasoning, and nutmeg. Cook, stirring occasionally, for 5 minutes. Reduce the heat to medium-low and add the eggs. Cook, stirring constantly, until the eggs are just set and soft-scrambled. Season to taste with salt and pepper.

Serves 6

2 to 3 tablespoons olive or vegetable oil

1½ pounds lean ground beef

1 medium onion, chopped

2 cloves garlic, minced

8 ounces mushrooms, sliced

1 package (10 ounces) frozen chopped spinach, thawed and squeezed dry, or 8 ounces fresh spinach, stemmed and chopped

½ teaspoon Worcestershire sauce

¼ teaspoon dried Italian seasoning

Pinch of ground nutmeg

6 eggs, lightly beaten

Salt and freshly ground black pepper

BAKED EGG BASKETS

STEVE MILLER, ENGINE 34

Steve is a native of the West Coast who surfs at Ocean Beach, right down the hill from Station 34, on his days off and worked in restaurants for years. He came up with this California-style take on eggs Benedict—spinach, crabmeat, and eggs baked in crispy phyllo cups, served in a nest of spinach—for an Easter brunch at Station 34, after seeing something similar on a cooking show. Steve likes to top it all off with a little homemade hollandaise sauce and also recommends shrimp or diced ham and Swiss cheese in place of the crabmeat.

Adjust the oven rack to the center position and preheat the oven to 350°F. Butter a 12-cup muffin pan.

Cover 7 of the sheets of phyllo dough with a slightly damp towel. Lay the 8th sheet on the work surface and brush it with some of the melted butter. Lay 3 more sheets over the first one, brushing each with butter before adding the next. Brush the 4th sheet with butter. Cut the stack of sheets into 12 squares, about 4½ inches on each side. Repeat with the other 4 sheets of phyllo. You should now have 24 stacks.

Press one of the stacks into one of the cups of the muffin pan. Press a second stack into the cup on top of the first at a 45-degree angle, using your fingers to make sure the phyllo stacks are pressed all the way into the cup. Repeat with the remaining stacks and cups.

continued on page 150

Serves 6

8 sheets phyllo dough (about 14 by 18 inches each), thawed

½ cup (1 stick) butter, melted

1 pound fresh spinach, stemmed and sliced into ⅛-inch ribbons

12 ounces crabmeat, picked over for shell fragments

2 tablespoons grated Parmesan cheese

12 eggs

Freshly ground white or black pepper

8 ounces cherry tomatoes, halved

Steve's Balsamic Vinaigrette (page 37)

Put 1 to 2 tablespoons of spinach in each cup, reserving the remaining spinach for serving. Distribute the crabmeat and Parmesan evenly among the cups, layering them on top of the spinach and pressing them gently into place. Crack an egg into each cup and season with pepper.

Bake until the eggs are soft-set and the phyllo cups are golden brown, 25 to 30 minutes. Divide the remaining spinach among 6 plates, making a nest with a hollow in the center. Scatter the tomatoes over the spinach and drizzle with the vinaigrette. Place 2 phyllo cups in the center of each nest. Serve immediately.

QUICK QUICHE with SPINACH, HAM, and MUSHROOMS

LT. ED DEA, DIVISION OF TRAINING

Make no mistake: Real firefighters do eat quiche. Especially when Ed's cooking. He calls this easy pie "a great way to use up leftovers." Try it with cooked chicken or turkey, too.

Adjust the oven rack to the center position and preheat the oven to 350°F.

Heat the oil in a heavy skillet over medium heat. Add the onion and sauté for 1 minute. Add the mushrooms and sauté for 3 to 5 minutes more, until the mushrooms are lightly browned and their liquid has cooked off. Transfer the mixture to a bowl and let cool for 10 minutes. Add the spinach and ham to the onion mixture, stirring to combine; spread the mixture evenly in the bottom of the pie shell. Sprinkle the cheese over the top.

In a medium bowl, whisk the eggs with the half-and-half, nutmeg, salt and pepper to taste and pour over the mixture in the pie shell. Bake for 25 to 35 minutes, until the center is firm and the top is lightly browned. Let cool for at least 10 minutes before slicing. Serve warm or at room temperature.

Serves 4 to 6

1 tablespoon olive oil

1 medium onion, diced

6 ounces mushrooms, sliced

1 package (10 ounces) frozen spinach, thawed, drained, and squeezed dry

4 ounces ham, diced

1 frozen pie shell (9 inches), thawed, or 1 unbaked pie shell (9 inches) made with No-Fail Piecrust (page 204), omitting the sugar

1 cup grated Cheddar or Gruyère cheese

3 eggs

1 cup half-and-half or whipping cream

Pinch of grated nutmeg

Salt and freshly ground black pepper

SIDES

SPICY GREEN BEANS
with BACON

MIKE GUAJARDO, ENGINE 16

"What can I say? Firefighters love hot food," says Mike, "and bacon . . . well, everybody loves bacon." Most of the work in this recipe can be done way ahead of time, so you can quickly finish the beans at the last minute. Look for chili oil in Asian markets or the ethnic foods section of most supermarkets, or substitute olive oil and a pinch of red pepper flakes.

Prepare an ice bath by filling a large bowl with water and ice. Bring a large pot of lightly salted water to a boil. Add the green beans and cook until crisp-tender, about 2 minutes. Using a slotted spoon, transfer the beans to the ice bath; this will stop the cooking process so that the beans remain crisp. When the beans have cooled, transfer them to a colander and allow them to drain completely. Spread them on paper towels to dry. Set aside.

Heat the olive oil in a large, heavy-bottomed skillet over medium heat. Add the onion and sauté until soft and translucent, about 3 minutes. Add the bacon and continue to cook for 5 minutes, or until the bacon is crisp and the onion is golden. Using a slotted spoon, transfer the bacon and onion to a plate lined with paper towels, leaving as much fat in the pan as possible. Discard the fat, wipe the skillet with a paper towel, and put the pan back on the heat. Add the chili oil and the green beans; sauté the green beans for 3 minutes. Toss in the bacon mixture, stirring until heated through. Season to taste with salt and pepper.

Serves 6

1 pound green beans, ends trimmed

2 tablespoons olive oil

1 medium yellow onion, diced

4 ounces thick-cut pepper bacon, diced

2 tablespoons hot chili oil

Salt and freshly ground black pepper

JALAPEÑO GREEN BEAN DELIGHT

DON VERANT, AIDE TO CHIEF MARIO TREVINO

Don concocted this spicy, colorful green bean dish, and he was so delighted with it, he said so in the name. And for good reason: Cooked in this way, green beans turn out bright green, crisp, and fresh-tasting. This technique works well with other vegetables, too, such as asparagus or broccoli. Zucchini is even easier. Just cut it into strips, skip the blanching step, and throw the strips right into the skillet, as you would the blanched beans. This recipe also has a surprise bonus: Chill the leftovers overnight, and you'll find you've made an equally "delightful" cold vegetable salad.

Prepare an ice bath by filling a large bowl with water and ice. Bring a large pot of lightly salted water to a boil. Add the green beans and cook until crisp-tender, about 2 minutes. Using a slotted spoon, transfer the beans to the ice bath; this will stop the cooking process so that the beans remain crisp and bright green. When the beans have cooled, transfer them to a colander and allow them to drain completely. Spread them on paper towels to dry. Set aside.

Heat the olive oil in a large skillet over high heat. Add the bell pepper strips and sauté for 1 minute. Add the garlic and jalapeño and sauté for 2 minutes more. Toss in the beans and cook for 3 minutes more, stirring continuously. Add the Tabasco sauce to taste and the sugar, if using. Stir in the olives and season to taste with salt and pepper.

Serves 6

1½ pounds green beans, ends trimmed

2 tablespoons olive oil

1 red or yellow bell pepper, stemmed, seeded, and cut into strips

3 cloves garlic, finely chopped

1 jalapeño chile, stemmed, seeded, and finely chopped

1 to 2 tablespoons green Tabasco sauce

¼ teaspoon sugar (optional)

½ cup black olives, pitted and coarsely chopped

Salt and freshly ground black pepper

DUDE'S GINGER CARROTS

FRANK HSIEH, ENGINE 41

Frank's love of surfing has earned him the nickname "Dude." And his love of carrots has made this recipe one of his trademarks. This is a family-friendly vegetable dish that you can put on the table without much effort by using packaged baby carrots. If they're not handy, just peel ordinary carrots and cut them into $1/4$-inch diagonal slices.

Serves 6

1$1/2$ pounds baby carrots
$3/4$ cup chicken broth or water
4 tablespoons ($1/2$ stick) butter
1$1/2$ tablespoons brown sugar
2 tablespoons grated fresh ginger
1 tablespoon chopped parsley or chives

Put the carrots, broth, butter, brown sugar, and ginger in a heavy-bottomed saucepan. Cover the pan and cook over medium heat until the carrots are crisp-tender, about 10 minutes. Remove the lid and cook, stirring, over medium-high heat until the liquid reduces to a syrupy glaze that coats the carrots, about 5 minutes. Toss with the parsley and transfer to a serving bowl.

Ginger Tips: *To peel ginger before grating, hold a sharp paring knife perpendicular to the ginger root and gently scrape the surface, being careful to remove only the paper-thin skin and not the most flavorful flesh just beneath it. For grating small amounts of ginger, a Japanese ceramic ginger grater is handy. Or try pressing small chunks of peeled ginger through a garlic press; you'll extract the juice, leaving much of the fibrous pulp behind.*

ROASTED ASPARAGUS
with TARRAGON

BARRY COMERFORD, ENGINE 7

This recipe works best with pencil-thin asparagus. It can also be prepared ahead of time, refrigerated, and served at room temperature; if you do make it in advance, wait till the last minute before adding the lemon juice so that the asparagus retains its bright green color.

Adjust the oven rack to the center position and preheat the oven to 450°F.

Trim off the tough ends of the asparagus spears and put the spears on a rimmed baking sheet. Sprinkle the olive oil, tarragon, and lemon zest over the asparagus and toss to coat evenly; arrange the asparagus in a single layer on the pan and season to taste with the salt and pepper. Bake for about 10 minutes, shaking the pan occasionally, until the asparagus is lightly browned but still crisp-tender. Remove from the oven and transfer to a serving platter. Drizzle with the lemon juice and serve immediately.

Serves 4

1 pound thin asparagus

2 tablespoons extra-virgin olive oil

2 tablespoons chopped fresh tarragon

1 teaspoon grated lemon zest

1 teaspoon coarse sea salt

Freshly ground black pepper

2 tablespoons freshly squeezed lemon juice

PROSCIUTTO-WRAPPED ASPARAGUS

PAUL CRAWFORD, ENGINE 35

If you're looking for a vegetable or first course to serve at a special-occasion dinner, try this. You can prepare everything in advance, all the way up to the baking stage, then bring it to room temperature and bake it just before serving.

Heat the butter and garlic in a small saucepan until the butter bubbles and foams. Turn off the heat and set the pan aside.

Trim off the tough ends of the asparagus spears. If they are fairly thick, peel the bottom half of each spear.

Prepare an ice bath by filling a large bowl with water and ice. Bring a large pot of lightly salted water to a boil. Add the asparagus and cook until crisp-tender, about 2 minutes. Using a slotted spoon, transfer the asparagus to the ice bath. When the asparagus spears have cooled, drain them in a colander.

Adjust the oven rack to the center position and preheat the oven to 375°F.

Cut the prosciutto slices into strips, about 1½ inches by 7 inches. Holding the short end of a strip of prosciutto about halfway up the tip of an asparagus spear, at a 45-degree angle, begin wrapping the prosciutto around the asparagus in a spiral along the length of the spear, leaving a bit of each end of the spear exposed. Repeat with the remaining asparagus, laying the wrapped spears in a casserole or baking dish large enough to hold them in a single layer.

Drizzle the garlic butter over the asparagus and sprinkle the cheese evenly over the top. Bake until the cheese is melted and the prosciutto is lightly brown, 12 to 15 minutes. Sprinkle the chopped parsley over the asparagus and serve immediately.

Serves 4 to 6

3 tablespoons butter

1 clove garlic, minced

1 pound asparagus

3 ounces prosciutto, sliced very thin

½ cup grated Parmesan cheese

2 teaspoons chopped Italian parsley

SPINACH and MUSHROOM SAUTÉ

MARTY VERHAEG, ENGINE 13

Marty learned this recipe from firefighter Jack Walker, but made it his own by adding the mushrooms. Try it with any of the more exotic mushrooms—shiitakes, oyster mushrooms, and diced portobellos—now available in most supermarkets.

Heat the olive oil in a large, deep-sided skillet or Dutch oven over medium-high heat and sauté the onion until lightly golden, about 5 minutes. Add the mushrooms and continue to sauté for 5 minutes more. Add the spinach and cook until slightly wilted, about 2 minutes. Stir in the broth concentrate and the Marsala, if using. Season to taste with salt and pepper. Serve immediately.

Engine vs. Truck: What's the difference between a fire engine and a fire truck? An engine is used to put out fires. It carries hoses, a supply of water, and a pump used to boost hydrant pressure. A truck is stocked with the tools, ladders, and equipment used to support the engine and perform search, rescue, and salvage operations. In San Francisco, an engine company consists of 1 officer and 3 firefighters, and a truck company has 1 officer and 4 firefighters.

Serves 6

2 tablespoons olive oil

1 medium yellow onion, diced

8 ounces brown (cremini) mushrooms, sliced or quartered

1 pound fresh spinach, stemmed

1 tablespoon granulated chicken or vegetable broth concentrate

1 tablespoon Marsala (optional)

Salt and freshly ground black pepper

COLESLAW with PINEAPPLE and DRIED CHERRIES

MARTY VERHAEG, ENGINE 13

The next time you're in the mood to make a batch of coleslaw, try Marty's sweet and tangy version. If you can't find dried cherries, substitute dried cranberries or golden raisins.

If using fresh pineapple, cut off the bottom and stand the pineapple upright on the cutting board. Holding the leaves firmly with one hand, cut away the skin in downward strokes. Remove the eyes by cutting shallow grooves diagonally along the sides of the eyes, following the natural spiral pattern. Cut the pineapple into 8 wedges and trim off the tough core edge from each wedge. Cut the pineapple wedges into ¹/₂-inch chunks and set aside.

In a large bowl, whisk together the mayonnaise and vinegar. Add the shredded cabbage, pineapple chunks, dried cherries, and green onions and toss to combine. Season to taste with salt and pepper. Let sit for 30 minutes or up to 1 hour before serving. Sprinkle the almonds over the top just before serving.

Toasting Nuts: *For best flavor, store untoasted nuts in an airtight container in the refrigerator or freezer and toast them just before you use them. To toast nuts: Preheat the oven to 350°F. Spread the nuts in a single layer on a rimmed baking sheet and bake for 5 to 10 minutes, stirring occasionally, until lightly browned. Spread the nuts out on a clean work surface to cool. Tip: Set a timer for 5 minutes and check the nuts every minute after it goes off.*

Serves 6

1 fresh pineapple or one can (20 ounces) pineapple chunks in syrup, drained

¹/₂ cup mayonnaise

¹/₄ cup red wine vinegar

¹/₂ medium head green cabbage, shredded

¹/₂ medium head red cabbage, shredded

¹/₂ cup dried cherries

2 green onions, white and pale green parts only, chopped

Salt and freshly ground black pepper

¹/₄ cup slivered almonds, toasted

NAPA CABBAGE SALAD

LARRY ZAMMARCHI, TRUCK 5

It all started with a recipe Larry got from his wife. He got lots of requests for it and began passing out copies. It spread like wildfire through the department, showing up under all kinds of names—Asian Slaw, Napa Slaw, "That Creamy . . . Chinese Cabbage Thing." And now, it's an SFFD institution.

To make the dressing: In a small bowl, whisk together the mayonnaise, sugar, vinegar, soy sauce, ginger, garlic, cayenne, and sesame oil.

To assemble the salad: Toss the cabbage, snow peas, radishes, green onions, and cilantro in a large bowl. Gently fold in the dressing. Refrigerate for 2 to 24 hours. Just before serving, sprinkle the almonds over the top.

Phoenix Rises to the Occasion: In a city surrounded by water on three sides, a boat can be the best way to fight a fire. When major water mains collapsed in the '89 earthquake, the fireboat Phoenix *pumped more than 5.5 million gallons of bay water to ten engines in the Marina, saving the neighborhood from devastation.*

Serves 6

DRESSING

1 cup mayonnaise

3 tablespoons sugar

3 tablespoons white wine vinegar

1 tablespoon soy sauce

1 tablespoon grated fresh ginger

2 cloves garlic, minced

$\frac{1}{4}$ teaspoon cayenne pepper

1 teaspoon Asian sesame oil

1 or 2 heads (about $3\frac{1}{2}$ pounds total) napa cabbage, halved, cored, and sliced crosswise into very thin strips

6 ounces snow peas, ends and strings removed, very thinly sliced on the diagonal (about $1\frac{1}{2}$ cups)

6 ounces radishes, thinly sliced (about $1\frac{1}{2}$ cups)

12 green onions, white and pale green parts only, sliced on the diagonal (about 1 cup)

1 cup chopped cilantro

$\frac{1}{2}$ cup slivered almonds, toasted (see page 163)

POTATOES FONTECA

PAULA CORCORAN, ENGINE 16

"I got this recipe from my sister," says Paula. "She and her husband always make it at every family gathering, and I've had good luck with it at the firehouse, too." It's an easy and flavorful twist on the usual roasted potatoes: First, they're roasted whole, then they're quartered and marinated with olive oil, garlic, and—here's the twist part—fresh mint. They're great with grilled steaks, lamb chops, chicken, or fish.

Adjust the oven rack to the center position and preheat the oven to 350°F.

Wash the potatoes, prick them in several places with a fork, put them in a baking dish, and roast them for 2 hours.

While the potatoes are roasting, mix the olive oil, garlic, mint, salt, and pepper to taste in a serving bowl big enough to hold the potatoes. Set aside.

Remove the potatoes from the oven. When they are just cool enough to handle, cut them into quarters and toss them with the olive oil mixture. Allow the potatoes to marinate for 30 minutes before serving. Serve slightly warm or at room temperature.

Serves 6

4 pounds medium red or white potatoes

1 cup extra-virgin olive oil

6 cloves garlic, chopped

1/2 bunch mint, leaves only, chopped (about 1 cup)

2 teaspoons kosher salt

Freshly ground black pepper

IRON SKILLET
SCALLOPED POTATOES

RICH WAGNER, ENGINE 10

"I've never been to cooking school," says Rich, "but I can imagine what it's like. I've been studying great cooks in the firehouse for years." It's been time well spent. His crispy-crusted skillet potatoes are tasty proof that scalloped potatoes don't have to be smothered in cream to be good.

Adjust the oven rack to the center position and preheat the oven to 350°F.

Use about 1 tablespoon of the butter to coat the inside of a 12-inch cast-iron or other oven-safe skillet. Combine the Gruyère and Parmesan in a small bowl.

Layer half of the white potatoes in the skillet. Season with salt and pepper. Spread half of the onion over the potatoes. Sprinkle one third of the cheese mixture evenly over the potatoes and onion. Repeat, layering on the red potatoes, salt, pepper, the remaining onion, and half of the remaining cheese mixture. Top with the remaining white potatoes. Put the skillet on the stove over medium-high heat and pour the broth over the potatoes. Press the potatoes down into the pan, season them with salt and pepper, and sprinkle the remaining cheese mixture over the top. Bring to a boil and cook for 3 minutes.

Drizzle the cream over the top of the potatoes and dot with the remaining tablespoon of butter. Place the skillet on a foil-lined baking sheet large enough to catch any drips. Bake until the top is nicely browned and the potatoes are tender when pierced with a knife, about 1 hour and 30 minutes. Remove from the oven and let sit for 15 minutes before serving.

Serves 6

2 tablespoons butter, at room temperature

1 cup grated Gruyère or Swiss cheese

½ cup grated Parmesan cheese

1½ pounds medium white or Yukon Gold potatoes, very thinly sliced

Salt and freshly ground black pepper

1 medium yellow onion, halved and thinly sliced

1 pound medium red potatoes, very thinly sliced

1½ cups chicken broth

2 tablespoons whipping cream

THREE-POTATO SALAD

LT. ED DEA, DIVISION OF TRAINING

The three potato varieties in this salad make a nice variation on an all-American summer barbecue classic. This salad can be made a day or two ahead of time and refrigerated until ready to use.

Place all of the potatoes in a large pot and cover with water. Lightly salt the water and bring it to a boil. Reduce the heat to medium-low and simmer until the potatoes are tender, 15 to 20 minutes. Drain the potatoes in a colander and allow them to cool. Cut the potatoes into 3/4-inch cubes.

In a large bowl, dissolve the sugar in the vinegar. Whisk in the mustard, mayonnaise, and relish. Add the celery, green onions, chopped eggs, and parsley, stirring to combine. Fold in the potatoes and season to taste with salt and pepper. Sprinkle with a little paprika just before serving.

Serves 6 to 8

1 pound Yukon Gold potatoes

1 pound red potatoes

1 pound white potatoes

Salt

1 tablespoon sugar

3 tablespoons distilled white vinegar

1 tablespoon prepared mustard

1 cup mayonnaise

2 tablespoons sweet pickle relish

3 stalks celery, diced

4 green onions, white and pale green parts only, chopped

3 hard-boiled eggs, peeled and chopped

1/4 cup chopped parsley

Freshly ground black pepper

Paprika

TORTILLA ESPAÑOLA

LT. JOSE LUIS VELO, ENGINE 39

In Spain, where Jose grew up, a tortilla is not a flatbread: It's a popular tapas snack—an open-faced omelet, usually made with potatoes and onions, that's eaten for breakfast with coffee, for lunch or dinner with a glass of beer or wine, or, as Jose says, "as a midnight snack, right from the refrigerator." His mom, Avela, taught him how to make this version. Serve it as a side dish or cut it into cubes, spear with toothpicks, tapas bar–style, and serve as an appetizer.

Heat 2 tablespoons of the olive oil in a 10-inch nonstick skillet over medium heat. Add half of the potato slices and cook, covered, for 10 to 15 minutes, until tender, stirring frequently. Remove the potatoes with a slotted spoon to a plate lined with paper towels and repeat the procedure with another 2 tablespoons of the oil and the remaining potatoes. Add the onion and the remaining 2 tablespoons oil to the same skillet and cook, covered, for about 10 minutes, stirring frequently. Remove the onion and set aside. Add the ham, if using, and cook until lightly browned, about 3 minutes; remove with the slotted spoon and set aside.

In a large bowl, beat the eggs lightly and fold in the potatoes, onion, ham, and parsley. Season with salt and pepper. Return the skillet, (which should still contain about a tablespoon of oil; if not, add oil accordingly) to medium-low heat. Add the egg mixture, spreading it evenly in the pan. Cook until the bottom is golden, about 5 minutes. To flip the tortilla, slide it onto a large plate, invert the skillet over it, and carefully flip the plate and skillet together. Place the skillet back on the heat and cook the second side of the tortilla until golden, about 5 minutes. Let the tortilla rest in the skillet off the heat for 5 minutes before sliding it onto a plate. When the tortilla has cooled to room temperature, cut it into wedges.

Serves 6

6 to 7 tablespoons olive oil

1½ pounds medium Yukon Gold potatoes, peeled and thinly sliced

1 large yellow onion, thinly sliced

4 ounces ham, diced, or Spanish-style chorizo, sliced (optional)

7 eggs

2 tablespoons chopped Italian parsley

Salt and freshly ground black pepper

ROASTED-GARLIC and SOUR CREAM MASHED POTATOES

FRANK HSIEH, ENGINE 41

Station 41 has its share of creative cooks. You're likely to spot a couple of well-thumbed food magazines on the dining room table, and the TV is often tuned to a cooking show. Frank has been known to try a dish five watches in a row until he gets it just the way he wants— or, as he puts it, "until someone objects, whichever comes first." He likes to serve these garlic mashed potatoes with roast lamb and Dude's Ginger Carrots (page 157). They're also good with a nice grilled steak.

Place the potatoes in a large pot with enough cold water to cover them by 2 inches. Add the 1½ tablespoons salt and bring to a gentle boil. Cook until the potatoes are tender when pierced with a fork. Drain the potatoes well in a colander, return them to the pot, and toss them over medium-low heat to dry them for about 1 minute. Transfer the potatoes to a large bowl. Heat the milk and the butter in a saucepan until the butter is melted. Add the hot liquid to the potatoes. Add the sour cream and roasted-garlic purée. Mash the potatoes with a potato masher or an electric mixer set on medium speed. Season to taste with salt and sprinkle the chives on top.

Serves 6

3 pounds russet potatoes, peeled and cut into 1-inch cubes

1½ tablespoons salt, plus more for seasoning

¾ cup milk or chicken broth

3 tablespoons butter

¾ cup sour cream

3 tablespoons roasted-garlic purée, squeezed from 1 large head roasted garlic

1 tablespoon minced chives

Roasted Garlic: *Roasting garlic produces a mellow purée that is good as a topping for* crostini *(slices of toasted crusty bread), as a sandwich spread, or as a seasoning for potatoes, grilled meat, dressings, soups, and sauces. Preheat the oven to 400°F. Slice the pointed end off of a large head of garlic, making extra cuts if needed on the side cloves to expose the tip of each (this will make it easier to squeeze out the garlic once it is roasted). Put the garlic on a piece of aluminum foil and drizzle it with 1 teaspoon of olive oil, turning it to coat well. Loosely wrap the garlic in the foil and roast it on a baking sheet for 40 to 50 minutes, until very soft and light brown. Let cool. Squeeze the garlic cloves from the skins into a small bowl and mash them with a fork to make a purée. You should have 2 to 3 tablespoons of roasted-garlic purée.*

TWICE-BAKED POTATOES

GEORGE JOSEPH PETTY III, ENGINE 23

These bacon-and-Cheddar-stuffed potatoes can be filled ahead of time and refrigerated, so all you have to do is pop them in the oven for their second baking while you're getting dinner ready.

Adjust the oven rack to the center position and preheat the oven to 400°F.

Wash and dry the potatoes, prick them in several places with a fork, and rub their skins with the melted butter. Wrap them individually in aluminum foil and bake for 1 hour. Reduce the oven temperature to 350°F and remove the potatoes from the oven. Let the potatoes rest until they are cool enough to handle.

While the potatoes are baking, fry the bacon in a medium skillet over medium heat until crisp. Using a slotted spoon, transfer the bacon pieces to a plate lined with paper towels. When the bacon has cooled, crumble it into small pieces

Remove the foil from the potatoes and cut them in half lengthwise. Using a soup spoon, scoop the pulp of the potatoes into a large bowl, leaving a thin shell of cooked potato inside the skin. Mash the pulp lightly with a fork, then add the sour cream, horseradish, green onions, cheese, and crumbled bacon; stir to combine well. Season to taste with salt and pepper. Fill the potato skins with the mixture and sprinkle each potato with a little paprika. Arrange the stuffed halves on a baking sheet; bake until the potatoes are heated through and the tops are lightly browned, about 25 minutes.

Serves 6

3 large russet potatoes (about 12 ounces each)

2 tablespoons butter, melted

4 ounces bacon, chopped

1/2 cup sour cream

1 tablespoon prepared horseradish

6 green onions, white and pale green parts only, chopped

8 ounces sharp Cheddar cheese, grated

Salt and freshly ground black pepper

Paprika

CREAMY POLENTA

To make great polenta, you need a nice heavy pot, a wooden spoon, and a strong forearm. The more you stir, the creamier it will be. You can serve it "straight up" with a little butter and Parmesan, top it with a stew, like Oxtail Ossobuco (page 67), or add all kinds of embellishments, such as roasted peppers (see page 141), roasted garlic (see page 170), sautéed mushrooms, pesto, ricotta, diced tomatoes, or olives. It can also be poured into a loaf pan or onto a board, allowed to cool until it's firm, and then sliced and grilled or used to make Polenta Lasagna (page 136).

Bring the broth, milk, and olive oil to a boil in a large, heavy-bottomed pot and reduce the heat to medium-low. Slowly pour in the polenta in a steady stream, stirring constantly with a whisk to keep lumps from forming. Reduce the heat to a simmer and cook for 20 minutes, stirring frequently with a wooden spoon. Stir in the butter and cheese. Season to taste with salt and pepper.

Ladder Lore: The ladders on San Francisco's fire trucks are famous in firefighting circles because they're made of wood. In fact, the department has its own woodworking shop in which the ladders are hand-built and maintained. They're works of art, but they're heavy. Firefighters have to demonstrate that they have the strength to carry them and set them up as part of their physical ability testing. Why not switch to light-weight metal? Because the city's narrow streets are crisscrossed with high-voltage electrical and trolley wires, making metal ladders too dangerous to use.

Serves 6

5 cups chicken or vegetable broth

1 cup whole milk

2 tablespoons extra-virgin olive oil

1 1/2 cups polenta

3 tablespoons butter

1/4 cup grated Parmesan, Romano, or Asiago cheese

Salt and freshly ground black pepper

STANYAN STREET FRIED RICE

JOHN HICKS, TRUCK 12

"I make this when I show up at work, open the fridge, and find a lot of leftovers from the watch before," says John. The same idea applies at home: Throw in some chopped cooked chicken, ham, or pork to turn this dish into a one-wok meal. If possible, make this recipe with day-old cooked rice, which is drier and separates better than freshly cooked rice when fried. Or do what John does at the firehouse: Cook the rice in the morning and refrigerate it for several hours before you use it.

Heat the vegetable oil in a medium nonstick skillet over medium heat. Add the eggs and fry them pancake style, flipping once, until golden brown on both sides. Transfer to a plate to cool. Cut the egg into 1/2-inch squares and set aside.

Remove the kernels from the ears of corn with a sharp paring knife, holding the tip of the ear on a cutting board and cutting downward along the ear.

Heat the sesame oil in a wok or large skillet over medium-high heat. Add the carrot and stir-fry for 5 minutes. Add the corn kernels and green onions and continue to stir-fry for 5 minutes more. Add the rice and stir to coat the grains in the oil; stir-fry for 3 minutes. Stir in the peas, chopped egg, soy sauce, and oyster sauce and stir-fry until warmed through. Sprinkle with the sesame seeds before serving.

Toasting Sesame Seeds: *To toast sesame seeds, put them in a dry, heavy-bottomed skillet over medium heat. Watch the pan carefully, stirring the seeds frequently to keep them from burning. When the seeds are golden and aromatic, spread them on a flat surface to cool.*

Serves 6

2 tablespoons vegetable oil

3 eggs, beaten

2 ears yellow or white corn

1/4 cup Asian sesame oil

1 carrot, peeled and diced

6 green onions, white and pale green parts only, cut into 1/4-inch slices

4 cups cooked white rice

1/2 cup frozen peas, thawed

2 tablespoons low-sodium soy sauce

2 tablespoons Asian oyster sauce

1 tablespoon sesame seeds, toasted, for garnish

MEXICAN RED RICE

BOB LOPEZ, TRUCK 9

Any time you see a Mexican recipe that says "serve with rice," this classic version will fill the bill. It's great for filling burritos, too.

Heat the oil in a large, heavy saucepan or Dutch oven over medium heat. Add the onion and garlic and sauté for 3 minutes, stirring occasionally. Add the rice and cook, stirring continuously, until the rice is a light golden color, about 3 minutes. Stir in the broth and tomatoes; season to taste with salt and pepper. Bring to a boil, then immediately reduce the heat to medium-low, cover the pot, and cook the rice for 20 minutes. Turn off the heat and allow the rice to rest for 5 to 10 minutes with the lid still in place. Fluff the rice with a fork and serve immediately.

Serves 6

¼ cup vegetable oil

1 medium yellow onion, diced

2 cloves garlic, chopped

2 cups long-grain rice

3½ cups chicken broth

1 can (14½ ounces) Mexican-style diced stewed tomatoes

Salt and freshly ground black pepper

PICO DE GALLO SALSA

ROBERT LUCHA, RESCUE 2

"To really make this the right way," says Robert, "the vegetables must be fresh from Casa Lucas and the chips from Casa Sanchez, both on 24th Street in the heart of the Mission District."

Combine the tomatoes, onions, cilantro, garlic, jalapeños, lemon juice, and lime juice in a large bowl. Season to taste with salt and mix well. Let stand for 1 to 2 hours to allow the flavors to come together.

Makes about 5 cups

6 large tomatoes, diced

3 medium white onions, diced

1 bunch cilantro, chopped

6 cloves garlic, finely chopped

3 jalapeño chiles, roasted (see page 141), stemmed, and finely chopped

Juice of 4 lemons

Juice of 1 lime

Salt

PINTO BEANS with GARLIC

BOB LOPEZ, TRUCK 9

Good news for time-pressed cooks: You can make a wonderful pot of traditional Mexican beans without soaking them overnight. The trick to achieving a soft, creamy texture is to simmer them very slowly. Salt them toward the end of the cooking so you can taste exactly how much salt to add.

Pour the beans onto a rimmed baking sheet and pick through them, discarding any small stones or foreign matter. Rinse the beans in a colander under cold water and place them in a large pot with the water, oil, onion, garlic, and bay leaf. Bring to a boil and reduce the heat to a very low simmer. Partially cover the pot and cook until the beans are tender, about 2 hours. Season to taste with salt and continue to cook for 15 to 30 minutes longer, until the beans are very soft and creamy. Discard the bay leaf and ladle the beans into individual bowls, or serve them family style directly from the pot at the table. If desired, crumble a little *queso fresco* over the beans and garnish them with a sprig or two of cilantro just before serving.

Serves 6

1 pound (2$\frac{1}{2}$ cups) dried pinto beans

8 cups water

3 tablespoons vegetable oil

1 medium white onion, diced

5 cloves garlic, chopped

1 bay leaf

1 to 2 teaspoons salt

GARNISHES

Queso fresco

Cilantro sprigs

"SMOKE and FIRE" BLACK BEANS STEVE FEINER, TRUCK 16

These spicy beans get their smoky flavor from two sources: ham hocks and a chipotle chile. Chipotles are jalapeños that have been smoke-dried. Look for them canned in adobo sauce *(en adobo)* in the Hispanic section of many supermarkets. If you've never cooked with chipotles, take it slow and start with only half the amount called for; their flavor can be, well, incendiary.

Pour the beans onto a rimmed baking sheet and pick through them, discarding any small stones or foreign matter. Rinse the beans in a colander under cold water and place them in a large pot with the water, ham hocks, onion, garlic, bay leaf, oregano, and chipotle. Bring to a boil and reduce the heat to a very low simmer. Partially cover the pot and cook until the beans are tender, about 2 hours.

Remove the ham hocks and, once they are cool enough to handle, pull the meat away from the bones, discarding the skin, bones, and fat. Shred the meat and add it to the beans. Season to taste with salt and continue to cook for 15 to 30 minutes, until the beans are very soft and creamy. Discard the bay leaf and ladle the beans into individual bowls, or serve them family style directly from the pot at the table.

Serves 6 to 8

1 pound (2 1/2 cups) dried black beans

8 cups water

1 pound smoked ham hocks

1 medium white onion, diced

5 cloves garlic, chopped

1 bay leaf

2 teaspoons dried oregano, preferably Mexican

1 canned chipotle chile *en adobo*

1 to 2 teaspoons salt

IRISH SODA BREAD

LT. ED DEA, DIVISION OF TRAINING

Irish firefighters made versions of this sweet-savory bread a fixture on San Francisco's firehouse tables more than a century ago, and it still turns up all the time. Ed's version is tasty right out of the oven, and, if there's any left over, he recommends it toasted and buttered with coffee in the morning. Once, when he was cooking for a big group of Firefighters' Toy Program volunteers, he scaled up the recipe to make a giant soda bread in an enormous industrial-sized skillet. It turned out great, but it was so big, he couldn't get it out of the kitchen without tearing it in two.

Adjust the oven rack to the center position and preheat the oven to 300°F. Butter the bottom and sides of a 10-inch cast-iron skillet and line the bottom of the skillet with a round of waxed paper or parchment. Lightly butter and flour the sides and bottom of the lined pan.

In a small bowl, coat the raisins with 1 tablespoon of the flour, separating any that are stuck together; set aside. Combine the remaining 4 cups flour with $1/2$ cup of the sugar, the baking soda, baking powder, salt, and caraway seeds in a large bowl.

In another large bowl, beat the eggs with the buttermilk and melted butter. Pour the mixture into the bowl containing the dry ingredients and mix until you have a smooth batter. Fold in the raisins and walnuts, if using. Pour the batter into the prepared skillet, level the top with a spatula, and sprinkle the remaining $1/2$ teaspoon of sugar over the top.

Bake for 1 hour, or until a toothpick inserted in the center of the bread comes out clean. Spread the 1 tablespoon butter over the top of the bread and let the bread cool in the pan for 10 minutes. Run a knife around the edge and invert the bread onto a serving plate. Remove the waxed paper and cool for 10 minutes more. Flip the bread over and serve warm with butter.

Makes one 10-inch round loaf

1 cup raisins

4 cups, plus 1 tablespoon all-purpose flour

$1/2$ cup, plus $1/2$ teaspoon sugar

1 teaspoon baking soda

4 teaspoons baking powder

$1/2$ teaspoon salt

$1 1/2$ tablespoons caraway seeds or anise seed

2 eggs

2 cups buttermilk

4 tablespoons ($1/2$ stick) butter, melted; plus 1 tablespoon, at room temperature

1 cup coarsely chopped walnuts (optional)

TUSCAN ROLLS

KAREN KERR, ENGINE 7

Karen is known for these hearty country-style rolls, and she loves to see the smiles on people's faces when she sets a warm, fragrant basketful on the table or uses them to make sandwiches. These are made with a double-rise yeasted dough, so you'll need to set aside some time to make them. But when you see those smiles, you'll be glad you did.

Dissolve the yeast and sugar in the warm water in a large mixing bowl; let stand for 5 minutes. Stir in the molasses, salt, whole-wheat flour, and 2 cups of the all-purpose flour. Gradually knead in the remaining flour until the dough holds together in a ball and no longer sticks to your hands. (The amount of flour you use will depend on the weather and humidity.)

Turn out the dough onto a lightly floured work surface and knead it for 5 to 10 minutes, pushing it away from your body with the palm of your hand. Or knead the dough using a stand mixer with a dough hook on medium-low speed for 5 to 10 minutes. Once the dough is kneaded, place it in the bowl, cover it with a towel, and let it rise in a warm place for 1 1/2 hours.

Transfer the dough to a lightly floured work surface and knead it briefly. Pat it into a circle and cut it into 4 equal pieces. Cut each of these into 6 equal pieces. Place these on baking sheets, spacing them 1 to 2 inches apart. Put the baking sheets in a warm place and let the rolls rise again for 30 minutes.

Adjust the oven rack to the center position and preheat the oven to 400°F.

Dust the rolls lightly with flour. Bake for 10 minutes, then reduce the heat to 350°F and bake for 12 minutes longer. The rolls are done when they are golden brown and sound hollow when tapped. Serve warm with butter or olive oil for dipping.

Makes 24 rolls

2 tablespoons (2 envelopes) quick-rising dry yeast

1 tablespoon sugar

5 cups warm water

1/4 cup molasses

2 tablespoons kosher salt

1 cup whole-wheat flour

10 to 12 cups all-purpose flour

GREEN CHILE and CHEESE CORNBREAD

LT. RICHARD BUSALACCHI, TRUCK 19

The next time anything with barbecue sauce is on the menu, try this moist, flavor-packed cornbread on the side. It's also the perfect match for Junkyard Dog Champion Chili (page 78) and a tossed green salad.

Adjust the oven rack to the center position and preheat the oven to 350°F. Lightly butter a 9-by-13-inch baking pan.

Beat the eggs in a large bowl. Stir in the corn, sour cream, and oil. Add the cornmeal, flour, baking powder, salt, and cumin, if using. Mix until all the ingredients are incorporated. Fold in the green onions, cheese, and chiles. Pour the batter into the prepared baking pan and bake until golden brown, 55 to 60 minutes. Remove from the oven and let rest for 15 minutes before serving. Cut into 12 squares and serve warm.

Serves 12

4 eggs

1 can (14$\frac{1}{2}$ ounces) creamed corn

2 cups sour cream

$\frac{1}{4}$ cup vegetable oil

1 cup yellow cornmeal

1 cup all-purpose flour

1 tablespoon baking powder

1 teaspoon salt

$\frac{1}{2}$ teaspoon ground cumin (optional)

6 green onions, white and pale green parts only, chopped

12 ounces sharp Cheddar cheese, grated

2 roasted poblano chiles (see page 141), stemmed, seeded, and diced, or 1 can (7 ounces) diced roasted green chiles

DESSERTS

PINEAPPLE UPSIDE-DOWN CAKE

LT. LOU BACCIOCCO, ENGINE 35

After 25 years of practice, Lou can make this cake in three sizes without a recipe, but we persuaded him to write it down. He notes that it's important to unmold the cake while it's still very hot. If you wait too long, the caramelized topping and pineapple will start to stick.

Adjust the oven rack to the center position and preheat the oven to 350°F. Lightly butter a 9-by-13-inch baking pan.

Cover the bottom of the baking pan with the brown sugar. Pour the melted butter over the brown sugar. Drain the pineapple slices, reserving 1/2 cup plus 2 tablespoons of the syrup, and place the slices over the brown sugar in even rows. Place a cherry half in each of the pineapple holes, with the cut side facing up. Sift together the flour and baking powder and set aside.

In a large bowl, using an electric mixer set on medium speed, beat the egg yolks with the granulated sugar for 3 minutes, or until thick. Add the reserved pineapple syrup and beat for 1 minute. Stir in the flour mixture until well incorporated.

Wash and dry the beaters; beat the egg whites in a large bowl on high speed for 3 to 4 minutes, until stiff peaks form. Using a rubber spatula, lightly fold the egg whites into the egg yolk mixture until just combined. Pour the batter over the pineapple slices and bake for 45 minutes, until the cake springs back when pressed.

While the cake is still hot, run a knife around the edges to loosen it from the pan, then place a serving platter or sheet pan over the cake and invert, unmolding the cake onto the platter. Any pineapple that sticks to the bottom of the cake pan can easily be replaced on the cake by pulling it off the pan with your fingers. Serve warm or at room temperature with vanilla ice cream.

Serves 8 to 10

1 1/2 cups dark brown sugar

1/2 cup (1 stick) butter, melted

1 can (20 ounces) pineapple slices in heavy syrup

6 maraschino cherries, cut in half

2 cups all-purpose flour

2 teaspoons baking powder

6 eggs, separated

2 cups granulated sugar

Vanilla ice cream for serving

LEMON MILK CAKE

LT. ED DEA, DIVISION OF TRAINING

This is the kind of cake you'd be proud to bring to a potluck or family dinner—straight-forward, satisfying, and just right with ice cream or fresh berries. If you're feeding a large group, you can double the recipe and bake it in a 9-by-13-inch pan.

Adjust the oven rack to the center position and preheat the oven to 350°F. Butter an 8-inch round cake pan. Line the bottom of the pan with a circle of parchment or waxed paper; butter the paper and dust the inside of the lined pan with flour.

To make the cake: Warm the milk, butter, and salt in a saucepan over medium heat, stirring occasionally, until the butter is melted. Combine the flour and baking powder in a small bowl. Beat the eggs with a whisk in a large bowl. Add the sugar and beat until incorporated. Add the hot milk mixture, a little at a time, beating after each addition. With a rubber spatula, stir in the flour mixture until just combined. Stir in the vanilla and lemon zest. Do not overmix. Pour the batter into the prepared pan and bake for 25 to 30 minutes, until a toothpick inserted in the center of the cake comes out clean.

While the cake is baking, make the syrup: Combine the lemon juice, sugar, and water in a small bowl, stirring until the sugar is dissolved.

Set the cake pan on a rack to cool for 10 minutes. Run a knife around the sides of the pan, cover the pan with a large platter, invert, and unmold the cake onto the platter; remove the paper from what is now the top of the cake. Poke a few holes in the top of the cake with a fork. Drizzle the lemon syrup over the cake and allow to cool. Just before serving, dust the cake with powdered sugar. Serve with vanilla ice cream.

Serves 6 to 8

CAKE

½ cup milk

2 tablespoons butter

½ teaspoon salt

1 cup all-purpose flour

1 teaspoon baking powder

2 eggs

1 cup granulated sugar

1 teaspoon vanilla extract

1 teaspoon grated lemon zest

LEMON SYRUP

⅓ cup freshly squeezed lemon juice (from 2 to 3 lemons)

⅓ cup granulated sugar

3 tablespoons water

Powdered sugar for dusting

Vanilla ice cream for serving

APPLESAUCE FRUITCAKE

LT. RICHARD BUSALACCHI, TRUCK 19

Like a great fruitcake, this recipe has been lovingly passed from hand to hand. It came to the firehouse by way of Richard's mother-in-law, Mary Asaro, who got it in 1950 from her friend Anna Dianda from New Orleans. If you're one of those people who thinks they don't like fruitcake, this might just be the one to win you over.

Adjust the oven rack to the center position and preheat the oven to 275°F. Butter and flour a 9-by-5-inch loaf pan.

Put the flour, granulated sugar, brown sugar, baking soda, cinnamon, and allspice in a large bowl; stir with a whisk to combine. Stir in the applesauce and vegetable oil. Gently stir in the raisins, candied fruit, walnuts, and almonds.

Pour the batter into the prepared pan and bake until the edges are set and the inside is still somewhat liquid, about 1 hour and 15 minutes. Cover the pan with foil and bake for about 15 minutes more, until a toothpick inserted in the center of the cake comes out clean.

Set the cake pan on a rack to cool for 10 minutes. Run a knife along the edge of the cake and unmold it onto the rack to cool completely.

Serves 6 to 8

2 cups all-purpose flour

$1/2$ cup granulated sugar

$1/2$ cup brown sugar

2 teaspoons baking soda

1 teaspoon ground cinnamon

$1/2$ teaspoon ground allspice

$1^1/2$ cups applesauce

$1/2$ cup vegetable oil

$1/2$ cup golden raisins

$1/2$ cup candied fruit, finely chopped

$1/4$ cup chopped walnuts

$1/4$ cup chopped almonds

WARM SWISS ALMOND APPLE CAKE

LT. RICHARD BUSALACCHI, TRUCK 19

Richard got this recipe from his mother-in-law, Mary Asaro, who suggests serving the cake warm. It's also good at room temperature (if there's any left over by the time it cools). Use full-flavored apples, such as Fujis, Granny Smiths, or Galas.

Adjust the oven rack to the center position and preheat the oven to 350°F. Butter and flour a 9-inch springform pan.

To make the cake: Combine the flour, baking powder, and salt in a bowl. Set aside. In a large bowl, using an electric mixer set on medium speed, beat the sugar and butter until light and fluffy, about 3 minutes. Add the eggs and lemon juice and continue to beat until well blended. Reduce the speed to low and gradually add the flour mixture, beating until well blended, about 3 minutes.

Spread the batter into the prepared baking pan. Carefully spoon the raspberry preserves over the batter. Arrange the apple slices over the top in a spiral pattern, pressing them lightly into the surface.

To make the topping: blend the almonds, sugar, sour cream, eggs, flour, and lemon zest, using a rubber spatula, until well combined.

Spread the topping evenly over the apples. Bake for 55 to 60 minutes, until the apples are tender and a toothpick inserted into the center of the cake comes out clean. Transfer to a rack and let cool for 10 minutes.

While the cake is cooling, prepare the glaze: In a small bowl, whisk together the powdered sugar and lemon juice.

To serve, run a knife around the edge of the cake. Carefully remove the side of the pan. Drizzle the glaze over the top and sides of the cake while it is still warm. Cut into wedges and serve immediately.

Serves 8

CAKE

2 cups all-purpose flour

2 teaspoons baking powder

1/4 teaspoon salt

2/3 cup granulated sugar

1/2 cup (1 stick) butter, at room temperature

2 eggs

2 tablespoons freshly squeezed lemon juice

1/4 cup raspberry preserves

3 to 4 tart apples, peeled, cored, and thinly sliced (about 3 1/2 cups)

TOPPING

1 cup sliced almonds

1/2 cup granulated sugar

1/2 cup sour cream

2 eggs, beaten

2 tablespoons all-purpose flour

1 teaspoon grated lemon zest

GLAZE

1/2 cup powdered sugar

2 teaspoons freshly squeezed lemon juice

CARROT-BANANA CAKE

BRENDAN CORMACK, ENGINE 44

What do you get when you cross a banana bread with a carrot cake? Brendan combined two of his favorite dessert recipes and found out: You get a super-moist, ultra-rich carrot cake! You can also make this recipe in a 9-by-13-inch baking pan.

Adjust the oven rack to the center position and preheat the oven to 350°F. Lightly butter a 10-inch (12-cup) Bundt pan.

To make the cake: Sift together the flour, cinnamon, baking soda, and salt into a bowl. Set aside.

In a large bowl, beat the eggs with the granulated sugar and brown sugar until smooth and creamy, using an electric mixer set on medium speed. Slowly drizzle in the vegetable oil while continuing to beat. Fold in the flour mixture. Stir in the carrots, pineapple, banana, and chopped pecans.

Pour the batter into the prepared baking pan and bake for 45 to 50 minutes, until a toothpick inserted in the center of the cake comes out clean. Remove from the oven and let cool on a rack.

While the cake is baking, prepare the frosting: Beat the cream cheese with the powdered sugar, butter, and cinnamon until smooth.

When the cake has cooled, invert it on to a platter and spread the frosting evenly over the top.

Serves 12

CAKE

2 cups all-purpose flour

1 tablespoon ground cinnamon

2 teaspoons baking soda

1/4 teaspoon salt

4 eggs

1 cup granulated sugar

1 cup brown sugar

1 cup vegetable oil

1 1/2 cups peeled and finely grated carrots (2 medium carrots)

1 can (8 ounces) crushed pineapple, drained

1/2 cup mashed very ripe banana (1 banana)

3/4 cup chopped pecans

FROSTING

8 ounces cream cheese, at room temperature

1 cup powdered sugar

3 tablespoons unsalted butter, at room temperature

1/4 teaspoon ground cinnamon

LEMON POUND CAKE

LT. ED DEA, DIVISION OF TRAINING

This rich pound cake is outstanding on its own and even better when you serve it with Warm Chocolate Sauce (facing page). A little ice cream or frozen yogurt and some strawberries on the side wouldn't be out of line either. Stored at room temperature in airtight plastic wrap, the cake stays moist and fresh-tasting for up to a week.

Adjust the oven rack to the center position and preheat the oven to 325°F. Butter and flour a 10-inch Bundt pan.

Using an electric mixer set on medium speed, in a large bowl beat the butter with the cream cheese until smooth. Slowly add the sugar and continue to beat until light and fluffy, about 5 minutes. Beat in the eggs yolks, one at a time, until well blended. Fold in the flour using a rubber spatula. Stir in the vanilla extract, almond extract, and lemon zest. Set aside.

In another large bowl, using clean, dry beaters, whip the egg whites with the salt until they form stiff peaks. Fold one fourth of the egg whites into the butter mixture to lighten it. Fold the butter mixture into the remaining egg whites just until combined. Do not overmix.

Spoon the batter into the prepared pan and tap the pan lightly on the counter to settle the batter. Bake until a toothpick inserted into the center of the cake comes out clean, about 1 hour and 15 minutes. Allow the cake to cool in the pan for 10 minutes before inverting and unmolding it onto a cooling rack.

Serves 8

1½ cups (3 sticks) butter, at room temperature

8 ounces cream cheese, at room temperature

3 cups sugar

6 eggs, separated, at room temperature

3 cups cake flour

2 teaspoons vanilla extract

½ teaspoon almond extract

2 tablespoons grated lemon zest

Pinch of salt

WARM CHOCOLATE SAUCE

JANICE HOAGLIN, ENGINE 40

Janice's sister-in-law, Bev, gave her the recipe for this foolproof chocolate sauce, which her family always makes at Christmas and serves over peppermint ice cream. Stored in an airtight container, it will keep for a week or more in the refrigerator.

In a medium, heavy saucepan over medium-low heat, stir the chocolate chips and butter until completely melted and combined. Whisk in the evaporated milk, then the powdered sugar and bring to a boil. Immediately reduce the heat to a simmer and cook, stirring constantly, for 2 minutes. Remove from the heat and let cool for 20 minutes; the sauce will thicken as it cools. Stir in the vanilla and salt; serve warm or at room temperature.

Zero Dalmatians: They may be a firehouse tradition in other cities, but there are no dalmatians—or, for that matter, dogs of any kind—in San Francisco's firehouses.

Makes about 2 1/2 cups

1 cup semisweet chocolate chips

1/2 cup (1 stick) butter, at room temperature

1 can (12 ounces) unsweetened evaporated milk

1 cup powdered sugar

1 teaspoon vanilla extract

Dash of salt

STRAWBERRY SHORTCAKE for a CROWD

LT. RICHARD BUSALACCHI, TRUCK 19

Strawberry shortcake is a crowd-pleaser. But making it for a crowd can be a challenge, especially if you have to assemble individual servings of crumbly biscuit-dough cakes. This recipe lets you have your cake and eat it, too. It's all done ahead of time, so all you have to do is bring it to the table and bask in the glory. The cake itself is a wonder: light and airy—like a cross between angel food and sponge cake—and just sweet enough to be the perfect match for berries and cream.

Adjust the oven rack to the center position and preheat the oven to 350°F. Line a 9-by-13-inch pan with aluminum foil, leaving some overhang; lightly butter and flour the lined pan.

To make the cake: Beat the egg yolks in a large bowl with an electric mixer set on high speed, until they are thick and pale yellow, about 3 minutes. Add the cold water and beat until thick, about 2 minutes more. Reduce the mixer speed to low and gradually mix in the sugar and vanilla. Using a rubber spatula, fold in the flour and salt.

Wash and dry the beaters; beat the egg whites on medium speed in a clean, dry bowl until foamy, about 1 minute. Add the cream of tartar, increase the speed, and beat until the whites form stiff peaks, about 5 minutes more. Gently fold the egg whites into the egg yolk mixture until just combined. Pour the batter into the prepared pan and bake for 35 to 45 minutes, until a toothpick inserted in the center of the cake comes out clean. Place the pan on a rack and let it cool to room temperature.

While the cake is baking, make the filling: Put the strawberries in a large bowl with the water and granulated sugar. Mix gently to combine; cover and refrigerate for 1 hour.

continued on page 196

Serves 12

CAKE

6 eggs, separated

1/2 cup cold water

1 1/2 cups granulated sugar

1/2 teaspoon vanilla extract

1 1/2 cups sifted all-purpose flour

1/4 teaspoon salt

3/4 teaspoon cream of tartar

FILLING

2 pounds strawberries, washed, hulled, and quartered

3/4 cup water

1/4 cup granulated sugar

2 cups whipping cream

1 to 2 tablespoons powdered sugar

Richard "The Baker" Busalacchi is an officer, which means he doesn't officially have to share in the cooking duties. But he loves to make desserts, so when he's on duty, chances are you'll find him in the kitchen anyway.

When the cake has cooled, whip the cream in a large, chilled bowl, using chilled beaters, until light and airy. Add powdered sugar to taste and whip for 30 seconds more.

To assemble the cake: Remove the cake from the pan by lifting the overhanging foil. Carefully peel away the foil. Holding a long, serrated knife parallel to the work surface, gently slice the cake in half lengthwise. Insert 2 metal spatulas into the cake to lift off the top layer and set it aside.

Drain and reserve the syrup that has formed in the bowl with the strawberries. Drizzle half of this syrup over the bottom layer of the cake. With a rubber spatula, spread half of the whipped cream evenly over the bottom layer, then distribute half of the strawberries over the whipped cream. Place the top layer of the cake on top of the strawberries, drizzle it with the remaining strawberry syrup, and spread the remaining whipped cream over the top. Arrange the remaining strawberries over the top of the cake. Let stand for at least 15 to 20 minutes, or up to several hours in the refrigerator, before serving.

CHOCOLATE CHIP CHEESECAKE ROBERT VIGIL, TRUCK 7

Cinnamon graham crackers are the secret to Robert's tasty cheesecake crust. You can replace the chocolate chips in this dense, rich cheesecake with white chocolate or butterscotch chips.

Adjust the oven rack to the center position and preheat the oven to 350°F. Lightly butter a 9-inch springform pan.

To make the crust: Combine the graham cracker crumbs and the melted butter in a large bowl. Press the crumb mixture onto the bottom and halfway up the sides of the springform pan. Set aside.

To make the filling: Beat the cream cheese with the sour cream in a large bowl until smooth, using an electric mixer set on medium speed. Add the sugar and beat until blended. Beat in the eggs, one at a time. Stir in the cream, vanilla, and 1 cup of the chocolate chips. Pour the mixture into the prepared crust. Scatter the remaining 1/3 cup chips over the top.

Bake until the cheesecake is set in the center, 40 minutes. Remove from the oven and cool on a wire rack for 30 minutes. Run a thin, sharp knife around the edge of the cake to loosen the crust from the pan. Cool for 30 minutes more. Cover with plastic wrap and refrigerate for 3 to 4 hours. When ready to serve, remove the side of the pan and slice the cake into wedges.

Serves 8 to 10

CRUST

1 3/4 cups finely ground cinnamon graham crackers (about 12 crackers)

1/2 cup (1 stick) butter, melted

FILLING

1 1/2 pounds cream cheese, at room temperature

1 1/2 cups sour cream

1 cup sugar

3 eggs

1/2 cup whipping cream

1 teaspoon vanilla extract

1 1/3 cups miniature chocolate chips

CRAZY CAKE

Just like Tim Callen's Five-Minute "Free Cake" (page 200), this is an almost impossibly easy, moist chocolate cake that you can probably make right now from ingredients in your kitchen. It's even good without the frosting. This is also a fun recipe to make with kids. "My mom, Frances Fava Gamick—who passed away the day before my final exam at the academy—made this all the time when I was growing up," says Paula. "Whenever I make it at the firehouse, I'm always reminded of her sweet spirit."

Adjust the oven rack to the center position and preheat the oven to 350°F. Butter a 9-by-13-inch baking pan.

To make the cake: Sift together the flour, sugar, cocoa powder, salt, and baking soda directly into the baking pan. Spread this mixture out evenly in the pan and make three "wells" in it. Into one well, pour the oil; into the second, pour the vinegar; and into the third, the vanilla. Pour the water into the pan. Mix with a fork until the dry ingredients are just incorporated; do not overmix. Place the pan in the oven and bake until the cake is just firm and a toothpick inserted in the center comes out clean, 45 to 50 minutes. Allow the cake to cool completely on a rack before frosting.

Meanwhile, prepare the frosting: In a large bowl, beat the cream cheese with an electric mixer on medium speed. Gradually beat in the powdered sugar and the cocoa powder.

Spread the frosting directly on the cake in the pan, or unmold the cake onto a large platter before frosting it.

Serves 8

CAKE

3 cups all-purpose flour

2 cups granulated sugar

6 tablespoons unsweetened cocoa powder

1 teaspoon salt

2 teaspoons baking soda

$1/2$ cup vegetable oil

2 tablespoons red wine vinegar

2 teaspoons vanilla extract

2 cups water

FROSTING

8 ounces cream cheese, at room temperature

8 ounces (about 2 cups) powdered sugar

3 tablespoons unsweetened cocoa powder

FIVE-MINUTE "FREE CAKE"

LT. TIM CALLEN, TRUCK 16

Firefighters share the cost of every meal they eat on the job, and whoever's on kitchen duty is responsible for keeping keep those costs under control. Tim does his bit by making this easy chocolate cake that can be thrown together from the "free" ingredients already on hand in just about any firehouse kitchen.

Combine the milk with the lemon juice and let stand at room temperature for 1 hour so that the milk curdles.

Adjust the oven rack to the center position and preheat the oven to 350°F. Butter a 9-by-13-inch baking pan.

Sift the flour with the cocoa powder, baking soda, sugar, and salt. Beat in the curdled milk, eggs, butter, and vanilla. Stir in the hot water until well combined. Pour the batter into the baking pan and bake for about 40 minutes, or until a toothpick inserted in the center comes out clean. Serve warm or at room temperature with ice cream.

Serves 6 to 8

1 cup milk

2 tablespoons freshly squeezed lemon juice

2½ cups all-purpose flour

⅔ cup unsweetened cocoa powder

2 teaspoons baking soda

2 cups sugar

½ teaspoon salt

2 eggs

¾ cup (1½ sticks) butter, melted and slightly cooled

1 teaspoon vanilla extract

1 cup hot water

Ice cream for serving

BROWN SUGAR–BERRY COFFEE CAKE

HEATHER BUREN, MEDIC 29

This is an old-fashioned streusel-topped coffee cake with a layer of berries hidden inside. If you can't find good fresh berries, use thawed individually quick-frozen (IQF) ones.

Adjust the oven rack to the center position and preheat the oven to 350°F. Butter and flour a 9- or 10-inch springform pan.

To make the topping: In a medium bowl, combine the brown sugar, granulated sugar, flour, walnuts, cinnamon, cloves, and nutmeg; using 2 knives, cut in the butter. Set aside.

To make the cake: Combine the flour, baking powder, and salt in a large bowl. In another large bowl, using an electric mixer set on medium speed, beat the butter and sugar until smooth, about 3 minutes. Beat in the eggs, one at a time, beating well after each addition. Beat in the vanilla. With the mixer on low speed, beat in the flour mixture in three additions, alternating with the milk and sour cream.

Pour half of the batter into the prepared pan. Spread the berries over the batter in an even layer. Pour the rest of the batter over the berries. Sprinkle the topping evenly over the batter.

Bake until a toothpick inserted in the center of the cake comes out clean, about 1 hour.

Set the cake pan on a rack to cool for 10 minutes. Remove the side of the pan and slice.

Serves 8

TOPPING

½ cup brown sugar

¼ cup granulated sugar

½ cup all-purpose flour

¼ cup finely chopped walnuts

2 teaspoons ground cinnamon

¼ teaspoon ground cloves

¼ teaspoon ground nutmeg

4 tablespoons (½ stick) butter, at room temperature

CAKE

2 cups all-purpose flour

1 tablespoon baking powder

½ teaspoon salt

½ cup (1 stick) butter, at room temperature

¾ cup granulated sugar

3 eggs

1 teaspoon vanilla extract

¾ cup milk

½ cup sour cream

6 ounces fresh blackberries, blueberries, raspberries, or a combination

ZUCCHINI BREAD

LT. RICHARD BUSALACCHI, TRUCK 19

Be prepared: People will take one bite of this rich, moist bread and ask you for the recipe. Richard says it's a great way to use up those giant homegrown zucchini his colleagues bring in to work all summer long. The recipe makes two loaves, so you can enjoy one and give the other to a friend—though once you taste it, you may not want to share.

Adjust the oven rack to the center position and preheat the oven to 350°F. Butter and flour two 4$\frac{1}{2}$-by-8$\frac{1}{2}$-inch loaf pans.

Sift the flour, baking soda, baking powder, cloves, cinnamon, and salt together into a bowl or onto a piece of waxed paper.

Using an electric mixer, beat the oil, sugar, eggs, and vanilla in a large bowl until smooth. Fold in the flour mixture. Fold in the zucchini and the walnuts, if using.

Divide the batter evenly between the pans. Bake until a toothpick inserted in the center of a loaf comes out clean, about 1 hour. Let cool on a rack for 30 minutes. Run a knife around the edges and carefully remove the loaves from the pans.

Makes 2 loaves

3 cups all-purpose flour

1 teaspoon baking soda

$\frac{1}{2}$ teaspoon baking powder

$\frac{1}{2}$ teaspoon ground cloves

1 tablespoon ground cinnamon

1 teaspoon salt

1 cup safflower oil

2 cups sugar

2 eggs, lightly beaten

1 tablespoon vanilla extract

2 cups grated zucchini (2 medium zucchini; about 9 ounces total)

1 cup walnuts, chopped (optional)

NO-FAIL PIECRUST

This pie dough comes together quickly in the food processor and is easy to work with. It can also be used for quiches and savory pies by simply omitting the sugar. The recipe makes enough for two pie shells. If you're making only one pie, make the whole batch anyway and freeze half for another time. Wrapped airtight, it will keep for up to two months.

Sift the flour with the salt and sugar into the bowl of a food processor. Distribute the pieces of butter and vegetable shortening over the flour. Pulse the machine a few times, until the mixture is the consistency of coarse meal. Add the ice water, a small amount at a time, pulsing until the dough begins to form a ball; you may not need all 8 tablespoons of water. Turn the dough out onto a clean work surface and divide it into 2 pieces. Form each piece into a flat disk, about 3/4 inch thick, and wrap the disks individually in plastic wrap. Refrigerate for 45 minutes. The dough can be frozen at this point for later use. Thaw frozen dough in the refrigerator for 24 hours before using.

Remove the dough from the refrigerator and discard the plastic wrap. Lightly flour the rolling pin and the work surface. Roll out the dough into a 12- to 13-inch round, giving it an occasional quarter turn so that its shape remains circular. The rolled dough should be large enough to leave a 1-inch overhang when it is pressed into the pie pan. Drape the dough over the rolling pin and carefully transfer it to the pan. Gather the overhang to form a rim and crimp it decoratively with your fingers. Prick the bottom and sides of the dough with a fork and place the shell in the freezer for 15 to 20 minutes before baking.

Makes two 9-inch pie shells

2 1/2 cups all-purpose flour

1/4 teaspoon salt

1 tablespoon sugar

1/2 cup (1 stick) butter, chilled, cut into 1/2-inch cubes

1/3 cup vegetable shortening, chilled, cut into pieces

7 to 8 tablespoons ice water

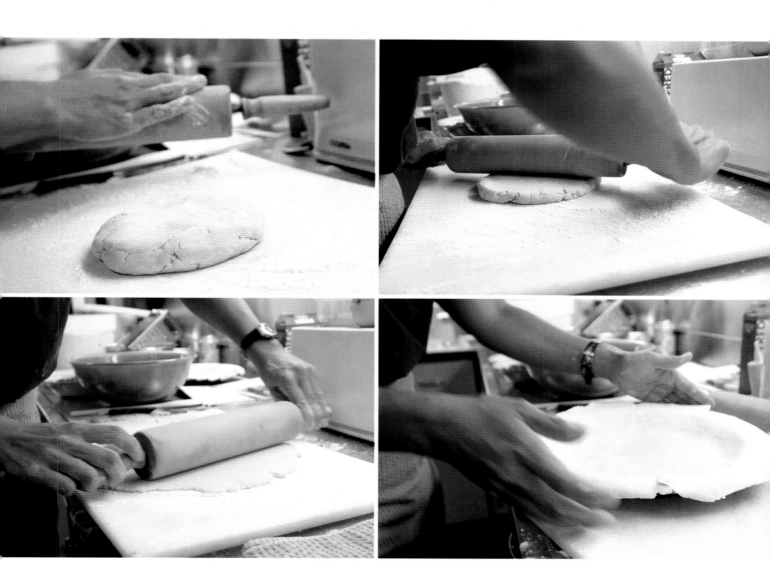

To prebake the pie shell (for recipes in which the filling is not baked): Adjust the oven rack to the center position and preheat the oven to 425°F. Line the pie shell with foil and fill it with pie weights or dried beans. Bake for 15 minutes. Remove the foil and weights and lower the oven temperature to 350°F. Bake for 12 to 15 minutes more, until the crust is golden brown. If the edges begin to brown too quickly, cover them with a strip of foil. Cool on a rack at room temperature before filling.

LEMON MERINGUE PIE

LT. RICHARD BUSALACCHI, TRUCK 19

This recipe is based on one Richard got from his mother, Lucille Busalacchi. It produces a textbook lemon meringue pie that stands tall, slices beautifully, and tastes like something you wish *your* mom used to make.

To make the filling: Separate 3 of the eggs into two large bowls. To the bowl with the yolks, add the remaining whole egg and the lemon juice; whisk to combine. Cover and refrigerate the whites for later use.

Whisk together the cornstarch, sugar, salt, and water in a heat-proof bowl. Set the bowl over a pot of boiling water over medium-high heat. Whisk in the egg yolk–lemon mixture. Continue whisking until the mixture thickens and comes together, about 10 minutes.

Remove the bowl from the heat and whisk in the butter and lemon zest. Let the filling cool for 15 minutes, then pour it into the prebaked pie shell. Cover the pie with plastic wrap and chill it in the refrigerator for 2 hours.

To finish the pie: Bring the egg whites to room temperature, adjust the oven rack to the upper third of the oven, and preheat the oven to 350°F.

Using an electric mixer, beat the egg whites with the cream of tartar in a large bowl. When the whites begin to hold their shape in stiff peaks, beat in the sugar, 1 tablespoon at a time. When the egg whites are stiff and glossy and you can no longer feel any grittiness from the sugar when you rub a bit of the whites between your fingers, spread the egg whites evenly over the top of the pie filling, using a rubber spatula to create raised peaks.

Serves 8

FILLING

4 eggs

1/3 cup freshly squeezed lemon juice

1/2 cup cornstarch

1 1/3 cups sugar

1/2 teaspoon salt

1 1/3 cups water

2 tablespoons butter, at room temperature

1 teaspoon grated lemon zest

1 pie shell (9 inches) made with No-Fail Piecrust (page 204), prebaked as directed and cooled

1/4 teaspoon cream of tartar

5 tablespoons sugar

Put the pie on a baking sheet and place it in the oven. Bake until the meringue is lightly browned, 10 to 15 minutes. (If the meringue sets but does not look sufficiently browned, place it under a preheated broiler. Leave the door open and watch the pie constantly, turning occasionally, until the meringue has browned evenly.) Allow the pie to cool completely before serving.

TANGY LEMON BARS

LT. RICHARD BUSALACCHI, TRUCK 19

Richard adapted these shortbread lemon bars from a recipe he was given by a favorite local café, the Home Sweet Home Tea Room in Santa Rosa, California.

Adjust the oven rack to the center position and preheat the oven to 350°F. Butter a 9-by-13-inch baking pan.

To make the crust: Using an electric mixer, cream the butter and powdered sugar in a large bowl until fluffy, about 2 minutes. Add the flour and continue beating until well blended. Transfer the mixture to the prepared baking pan and use your fingers to press it evenly over the bottom of the pan. Bake for 20 minutes.

While the crust is baking, prepare the topping: Using an electric mixer set on medium speed, beat the eggs until light and foamy in a medium bowl. Gradually add the granulated sugar and beat until the mixture is thick and pale yellow in color. Add the lemon juice, lemon zest, flour, and baking powder; beat until thoroughly blended.

Pour the topping over the warm, baked crust and sprinkle the pistachios, if using, over the top. Bake for 25 minutes, until the topping is set and lightly browned. Remove the pan from the oven and allow it to cool completely on a rack. Slice into bars or squares. Dust with powdered sugar.

Makes eighteen 2-by-3-inch bars

CRUST

1 cup (2 sticks) butter, at room temperature

1/2 cup powdered sugar

2 cups all-purpose flour

TOPPING

4 eggs

1 1/2 cups granulated sugar

1/2 cup freshly squeezed lemon juice

2 tablespoons grated lemon zest

1/3 cup all-purpose flour

1 teaspoon baking powder

1/2 cup chopped pistachios (optional)

1 to 2 tablespoons powdered sugar for dusting

APPLE WALNUT CRISP

LT. JEANNE SEYLER, ENGINE 29

Even the most confirmed nonbaker can make a crisp, and as crisps go, this one is particularly forgiving. Serve it warm with ice cream or whipped cream. To make it extra-special, warm some caramel sauce with a pinch of cinnamon to drizzle over each serving.

Adjust the oven rack to the center position and preheat the oven to 375°F. Butter a 9-by-13-inch baking pan.

To make the topping: Combine the flour, granulated sugar, walnuts, and cinnamon in a large bowl. Add the butter and use your fingers to work it into the flour mixture.

To make the filling: In another large bowl, toss the apples with the brown sugar, flour, lemon juice, lemon zest, cinnamon, and nutmeg.

Pour the apple mixture into the prepared pan, spreading it evenly. Crumble the topping mixture over the apples. Bake until the apples are soft and the topping is golden brown, about 45 minutes. Cool on a rack for at least 10 minutes. Serve warm or at room temperature with ice cream.

Serves 6 to 8

TOPPING

1½ cups all-purpose flour

½ cup granulated sugar

½ cup chopped walnuts

1 teaspoon ground cinnamon

¾ cup (1½ sticks) butter, chilled, cut into ½-inch cubes

FILLING

6 medium Granny Smith or other tart apples, peeled, cored, and sliced (about 6 cups)

¾ cup brown sugar

3 tablespoons all-purpose flour

1 tablespoon lemon juice

1 teaspoon grated lemon zest

1 teaspoon ground cinnamon

¼ teaspoon ground nutmeg

Vanilla ice cream or frozen yogurt for serving

CHOCOLATE CREAM PIE

LT. RICHARD BUSALACCHI, TRUCK 19

An easy, densely chocolaty pie with a no-bake filling. If you're in a hurry, you can pop the just-filled pie in the freezer to make the filling set faster.

To make the filling: Melt the chocolate in the microwave using low power or in the top of a double-boiler or heatproof bowl set over a pot of warm water with the burner set to medium-low. In a large bowl, using an electric mixer set on medium speed, beat the powdered sugar and butter until light and fluffy, about 3 minutes. Beat in the melted chocolate and vanilla. Add the eggs, one at a time, beating well after each addition until thoroughly combined.

Pour the filling into the pie shell, cover with aluminum foil, and place in the refrigerator for 4 hours, until the filling is set and completely chilled.

Just before serving, remove the pie from the refrigerator and uncover it. Whip the cream until it begins to thicken, then gradually add the powdered sugar to taste and the vanilla; continue whipping until stiff peaks form. Spread the whipped cream over the pie. Use a vegetable peeler to shave some chocolate over the pie as a garnish.

Serves 8

FILLING

6 ounces semisweet chocolate

1 cup powdered sugar

1/2 cup (1 stick) butter, at room temperature

1 teaspoon vanilla extract

4 eggs

1 pie shell (9 inches) made with No-Fail Piecrust (page 204), prebaked as directed and cooled

1 cup whipping cream

2 to 3 teaspoons powdered sugar

1 teaspoon vanilla extract

1 ounce semisweet chocolate for garnish

TIRAMISÙ

In 2001, when he was a probie at Station 16, Derio was assigned the weighty responsibility of providing dessert for the crew's Thanksgiving dinner. He called his mom, Maria, who is from Calabria and had worked as a baker at Dianda's and Victoria Pastry, two famed North Beach Italian pastry shops. This is the family recipe she gave him (although her version was written in Italian). Derio no longer works at Station 16, but they're still talking about his mom's tiramisù.

Beat the egg yolks and sugar in a large bowl, using an electric mixer set on medium speed, until the mixture is creamy and pale yellow, about 4 minutes. Beat in the mascarpone.

In a large bowl, using clean, dry beaters, whip the egg whites until frothy, add the salt, and beat on high speed until stiff peaks form, about 3 minutes. Fold one fourth of the egg whites into the yolk mixture, then gently fold the yolk mixture into the whites until well combined. Spread one fourth of this mixture evenly on the bottom of a 9-by-13-inch glass baking dish.

Combine the coffee and Marsala in a wide, shallow bowl. Dip a sheet of ladyfingers very quickly into the coffee mixture; layer the soaked ladyfingers on top of the mascarpone mixture in the dish. Repeat this process until you have covered the mascarpone mixture with a layer of ladyfingers. Spread another fourth of the mascarpone mixture evenly over the ladyfingers. Top with a second layer of ladyfingers and another fourth of the mascarpone mixture. Top with a third layer of ladyfingers and the remaining mascarpone mixture.

Sift the cocoa over the top. Refrigerate for at least 4 hours and up to 24 hours. Just before serving, use a vegetable peeler to shave the chocolate over the top.

Serves 8

6 eggs, separated

¼ cup sugar

1½ pounds mascarpone cheese

Pinch of salt

3 cups strong coffee, at room temperature

3 tablespoons Marsala

15 to 24 ounces (about 100) ladyfingers

1 tablespoon unsweetened cocoa powder for dusting

1 ounce semisweet chocolate for garnish

SAN FRANCISCO
CHOCOLATE CHIP COOKIES

ANNIE HODDINOTT, ENGINE 9

Annie got this recipe from Kathy Gilbraith, a medic from Station 28. "I'm English, so I know nothing whatsoever about cooking," Annie says with a wink. "But this is the one recipe I can recite by heart and love to make, because you just toss everything together in a bowl." She likes to make the dough in the morning and bake a batch or two later to go with a midafternoon card game. And she insists that locally made Guittard chocolate chips are a must, because "that's the San Francisco part."

Put the granulated sugar, brown sugar, flour, egg, baking soda, vanilla, and butter in a large bowl. Blend well, using an electric mixer set on medium speed. Fold in the chocolate chips and refrigerate the dough for at least 30 minutes.

Adjust the oven rack to the center position and preheat the oven to 350°F. Lightly butter 2 baking sheets.

Roll the dough into 24 golf ball–sized pieces. Place on the baking sheets and press into flat, even disks, about 3 inches in diameter, leaving about 2 inches of space between them. Bake until golden brown, 13 to 15 minutes.

Makes 2 dozen 4-inch cookies

3/4 cup granulated sugar

3/4 cup brown sugar

2 cups all-purpose flour

1 egg

1 teaspoon baking soda

1 teaspoon vanilla extract

1 cup (2 sticks) butter, at room temperature

2 cups (one 10-ounce package) giant chocolate chips, preferably Guittard

WALNUT BISCOTTI

ALISON YEE, ENGINE 12

Alison loves to bake. Even when it's not her official day in the kitchen, she'll often sneak in and whip something up to go along with the meal. Her biscotti always get a great reception. She notes that you can substitute whole almonds, raisins, or chocolate chips (in which case, omit the anise seed) for the walnuts.

Adjust the oven rack to the center position and preheat the oven to 350°F. Butter a baking sheet.

Whisk the flour with the baking powder in a large bowl; set aside.

Beat the eggs and sugar in another large bowl, using an electric mixer set on medium speed. Add the melted butter and vanilla and mix to combine. Gradually add the flour mixture, about a cup at a time, blending well after each addition.

Gently stir in the walnuts and anise seed, using a rubber spatula. You should now have a stiff dough that holds together and is only slightly sticky. If it is too sticky to work with, add a small amount of flour. Divide the dough into 6 equal portions. With lightly floured hands, roll each portion into a "log" about 1 inch by 5 inches.

Space the logs at least 2 inches apart on the baking sheet. Bake for 20 to 25 minutes, until the logs are golden and the surface springs back when pressed lightly. Cool in the pan on a rack for 5 minutes.

Carefully transfer the still-warm logs to a cutting board and cut them on the diagonal into ½-inch slices, using a serrated knife. Transfer the sliced cookies back to the baking sheet, placing them cut-side down; they will be somewhat fragile at this stage. Bake for 10 minutes. Remove the baking sheet from the oven, turn the cookies so that the other cut side is facing up, and bake for 10 minutes more, until golden brown. Transfer to a rack to cool.

Makes about 4 dozen cookies

3 cups all-purpose flour

1 heaping teaspoon baking powder

3 eggs

1 cup sugar

½ cup (1 stick) butter, melted

1 teaspoon vanilla extract

1 cup walnut pieces

1½ teaspoons anise seed

INDEX

A

Abella, Larry, 91
Almonds
    Caramelized Almonds, 34
    Warm Swiss Almond Apple Cake, 189
Anchovies
    Firehouse Caesar Salad, 46
    Pasta Puttanesca, 130
"Any Kind of Meat" Marinade, 101
Apples
    Applesauce Fruitcake, 187
    Apple Walnut Crisp, 209
    Warm Swiss Almond Apple Cake, 189
Artichokes
    Artichoke and Mushroom Focaccia, 144
    Penne with Chicken and Artichokes, 139
Asparagus
    Prosciutto-Wrapped Asparagus, 160
    Roasted Asparagus with Tarragon, 158
    Tim's Louis Salad, 48–49

B

Bacciocco, Lou, 185
Bacon
    Matt's Sauerkraut Sausage Surprise, 88
    Red Gumbo, 82–83
    Rigatoni alla Carbonara, 135
    Spicy Green Beans with Bacon, 155
    Twice-Baked Potatoes, 171
Baked Egg Baskets, 148–50
Baked Salmon Fillet with a Potato Chip
    Crust, 119
Banana Cake, Carrot-, 190
Barley Soup, Beef, 55
Beans
    Jalapeño Green Bean Delight, 156

Pinto Beans with Garlic, 175
    "Smoke and Fire" Black Beans, 176
    Spicy Green Beans with Bacon, 155
Béchamel Sauce, 138
Beef
    Beef Barley Soup, 55
    Caldo de Res, 53
    C-Watch Fried Mein with Oyster Sauce
        Beef, 132–33
    Grandma Milici's Spaghetti and
        Meatballs, 128–29
    Joe's Special, 147
    Junkyard Dog Champion Chili, 78–79
    Oxtail Ossobuco, 67
    Pot Roast with Red Sauce, 66
    Tamale Pie, 85
Beere, Mike, 45
Beet Salad, Roasted, with Raspberry
    Balsamic Vinaigrette, 51
Bell peppers
    Calamari Salad, 41
    Polenta with Sausage and Roasted
        Peppers, 140
    roasting, 141
    Swoop Stew, 71
Berry Coffee Cake, Brown Sugar-, 201
Biscotti, Walnut, 214
Blackened Red Snapper, 126
Blackening Rub, 126
Bob's Oven-Fried Chicken, 95
Bogue, John, Sr., 48
Bright, Dan, 70
Brooks, Worthy, 82
Brown Sugar-Berry Coffee Cake, 201
Bryant, Ed, 126
Buren, Heather, 201

Busalacchi, Richard, 144, 181, 187, 189, 195–96,
    203, 206, 208, 210
Buttermilk Ranch Dressing, 39
Buz's Perfect Fried Chicken, 94

C

Cabbage
    Coleslaw with Pineapple and Dried
        Cherries, 163
    Napa Cabbage Salad, 164
Caesar Salad, Firehouse, 46
Cakes
    Applesauce Fruitcake, 187
    Brown Sugar-Berry Coffee Cake, 201
    Carrot-Banana Cake, 190
    Chocolate Chip Cheesecake, 197
    Crazy Cake, 198
    Five-Minute "Free Cake," 200
    Lemon Milk Cake, 186
    Lemon Pound Cake, 192
    Pineapple Upside-Down Cake, 185
    Strawberry Shortcake for a Crowd, 195–96
    Warm Swiss Almond Apple Cake, 189
Calamari Salad, 41
Caldo de Res, 53
California Chicken Adobo, 91
Callen, Tim, 48, 200
Campanali, Mike, 117
Camp Blaze, 137
Cannon, Larry, 86
Carion, Michael, 61, 124
Carrots
    Carrot-Banana Cake, 190
    Dude's Ginger Carrots, 157
Cheesecake, Chocolate Chip, 197
Cherries, Dried, Coleslaw with Pineapple
    and, 163

Chicken
    Bob's Oven-Fried Chicken, 95
    Buz's Perfect Fried Chicken, 94
    California Chicken Adobo, 91
    Chicken and Chorizo Enchiladas, 104–5
    Chicken and Pork Pozole, 86–87
    Chicken Giovacchini, 110–11
    Chicken in a Barrel, 92–93
    Chicken Relleno, 106–7
    Chinese Chicken Salad, 36
    Home-Style Jook, 61
    Mexican Chicken Salad, 42
    Penne with Chicken and Artichokes, 139
    Polynesian Basting Sauce, 103
    Red Gumbo, 82–83
    Rosemary-Garlic Roast Chicken, 108
    Skillet Paella, 90
    Thai BBQ Chicken with Peanut Sauce, 96–97
    Thai Coconut Chicken, 112
    Tortilla Soup, 56
    Villa Gumbo, 84
Chiles
    chipotle, 176
    Green Chile and Cheese Cornbread, 181
    Jalapeño Green Bean Delight, 156
    Pico de Gallo Salsa, 174
    roasting, 141
Chili
    Chili Verde, 81
    Junkyard Dog Champion Chili, 78–79
Chinese Chicken Salad, 36
Chocolate
    Chocolate Chip Cheesecake, 197
    Chocolate Cream Pie, 210
    Crazy Cake, 198
    San Francisco Chocolate Chip Cookies, 212
    Warm Chocolate Sauce, 193
Chung, John, 58, 59, 132, 133
Cilantro-Sour Cream Dressing, 43
Cioppino, Firehouse 11, 120
Clams
    Firehouse 11 Cioppino, 120
    Red Gumbo, 82–83
    Skillet Paella, 90

Clifford, John, 45
Coconut milk
    Green Curry Salmon, 122
    Peanut Dipping Sauce, 96–97
    Thai Coconut Chicken, 112
Coleslaw with Pineapple and Dried
    Cherries, 163
Comerford, Barry, 126, 158
Cookies
    San Francisco Chocolate Chip Cookies, 212
    Tangy Lemon Bars, 208
    Walnut Biscotti, 214
Corcoran, Paula, 165, 198
Cormack, Brendan, 190
Corn. *See also* Hominy; Polenta
    Caldo de Res, 53
    Green Chile and Cheese Cornbread, 181
    Stanyan Street Fried Rice, 173
    Tamale Pie, 85
    Tortilla Soup, 56
Costa, Bob, 15, 92
Crab
    Baked Egg Baskets, 148–50
    Dungeness Crab Cakes, 127
    Firehouse 11 Cioppino, 120
    preparing cooked, 83
    Red Gumbo, 82–83
    Skillet Paella, 90
    Tim's Louis Salad, 48–49
Cranberries, Dried, Mixed Greens with
    Pears and, 52
Crawford, Paul, 160
Crazy Cake, 198
Creamy Polenta, 172
Crisp, Apple Walnut, 209
C-Watch Fried Mein with Oyster Sauce
    Beef, 132–33

D
Dair, Darryl, 90, 120, 127
Dalmatians, 193
Dea, Ed, 66, 103, 151, 167, 177, 186, 192
Dito, Derio, 211
Dogs, 193

Door slammers, 67
Duck Wonton Soup, 58–60
Dude's Ginger Carrots, 157
Dungeness Crab Cakes, 127

E
Ed's Tartar Sauce, 103
Eggs
    Baked Egg Baskets, 148–50
    Joe's Special, 147
    Quick Quiche with Spinach, Ham, and
      Mushrooms, 151
    Tortilla Española, 168
Enchiladas, Chicken and Chorizo, 104–5

F
Feiner, Steve, 38, 98, 176
Fireboat BBQ Sauce, 102
Fireboats, 164
Fire engines and trucks, 161
Firehouse Caesar Salad, 46
Firehouse 11 Cioppino, 120
"A Fireman's Prayer," 25
Fish
    Baked Salmon Fillet with a Potato Chip
      Crust, 119
    Blackened Red Snapper, 126
    Firehouse 11 Cioppino, 120
    Green Curry Salmon, 122
    Pacific Fish Tacos, 115–16
    Stuffed Sole Fillets, 121
    Villa Gumbo, 84
    Whole Roasted Salmon with Lemon-
      Basil Teriyaki, 117
Five-Minute "Free Cake," 200
Focaccia, Artichoke and Mushroom, 144
Frying tips, 116

G
Garlic, roasting, 170
Gibson, Rich, 84
Gilbraith, Kathy, 212
Ginger, preparing, 157
Giovacchini, Larry, 110

Grandma Milici's Spaghetti and Meatballs, 128–29
Green Chile and Cheese Cornbread, 181
Green Curry Salmon, 122
Grilling
    marinades and sauces, 101–3
    tips, 98–100
    tools, 100
Grocery shopping, 20–21
Guajardo, Mike, 23, 45, 65, 101, 155
Gumbo
    Red Gumbo, 82–83
    Villa Gumbo, 84

H
Ham
    Prosciutto-Wrapped Asparagus, 160
    Quick Quiche with Spinach, Ham, and Mushrooms, 151
    "Smoke and Fire" Black Beans, 176
Harrell, Jason, 67, 140
Hicks, John, 45, 173
Higgins, Joe, 103
Hill houses, 53
Hoaglin, Janice, 193
Hoddinott, Annie, 212
Home-Style Jook, 61
Hominy
    Chicken and Pork Pozole, 86–87
    purchasing, 86
Honey-Dill Vinaigrette, 38
Honey-Mustard Marinade, 102
Hsieh, Frank, 157, 170
Hunter, Sheila, 24, 108

I
Imbellino, Bob, 95
Irish Soda Bread, 177
Iron Skillet Scalloped Potatoes, 166

J
Jalapeño Green Bean Delight, 156
James (Station 16), 25
Joe's Special, 147

Johnson, Rich, 53, 115
Jones, Albert, 136
Jook, Home-Style, 61
Junkyard Dog Champion Chili, 78–79

K
Kalua Pig, 70
Kerr, Karen, 136, 137, 178
Kitchen duty, 13–15, 18–19
Kung Pao Prawns, 124
Kwan, Norm, 132

L
Ladders, 172
Lasagna, Polenta, 136, 138
Lemons
    Lemon Meringue Pie, 206–7
    Lemon Milk Cake, 186
    Lemon Pound Cake, 192
    Lemon Syrup, 186
    Tangy Lemon Bars, 208
Lopez, Bob, 74, 76, 81, 104, 105, 174, 175
Louis Salad, Tim's, 48–49
Lucha, Robert, 174

M
Marinara Sauce, 136
Marini, Tom, 85
Masa dough, 77
Matt's Sauerkraut Sausage Surprise, 88
McCulloch, Trace, 18, 51, 52, 139
Meatballs, Grandma Milici's Spaghetti and, 128–29
Meatloaf, Turkey, 113
Merrill, Cliff, 45, 143
Mexican Chicken Salad, 42
Mexican Red Rice, 174
"Mexican Restaurant" Salad, 43
Milici, Robert, 128–29
Miller, Steve, 37, 101, 148
Mixed Greens with Pears and Dried Cranberries, 52
Mom's Tamales, 74, 77

Mushrooms
    Artichoke and Mushroom Focaccia, 144
    Chicken Giovacchini, 110–11
    Chicken Relleno, 106–7
    Green Curry Salmon, 122
    Joe's Special, 147
    Polenta Lasagna, 136, 138
    Quick Quiche with Spinach, Ham, and Mushrooms, 151
    Rigatoni alla Carbonara, 135
    Spinach and Mushroom Sauté, 161
    Stuffed Sole Fillets, 121
    Swoop Stew, 71

N
Napa Cabbage Salad, 164
Newman, Denise, 55
Nielsen, Curt "Swoop," 14, 71
No-Fail Piecrust, 204–5
Noodles. See Pasta and noodles
Nuts, toasting, 163

O
Okra
    Red Gumbo, 82–83
    Villa Gumbo, 84
Olives
    Jalapeño Green Bean Delight, 156
    Pasta Puttanesca, 130
    Tamale Pie, 85
Oranges
    Orange and Ginger Grilled Pork Tenderloin, 65
    Orange-Ginger Sauce, 65
    Slug Salad, 34
    Yucatán Marinade, 101
Orengo, Buz, 94
Oxtail Ossobuco, 67

P
Pacific Fish Tacos, 115–16
Paella, Skillet, 90
Papera, Mike, 78

Pasta and noodles
 C-Watch Fried Mein with Oyster Sauce Beef, 132–33
 Firehouse 11 Cioppino, 120
 Grandma Milici's Spaghetti and Meatballs, 128–29
 Pasta Puttanesca, 130
 Penne with Chicken and Artichokes, 139
 Pot Roast with Red Sauce, 66
 Rigatoni alla Carbonara, 135
Peanut Dipping Sauce, 96–97
Pears, Mixed Greens with Dried Cranberries and, 52
Penne with Chicken and Artichokes, 139
Peppers, Roasting, 141
Petty, George Joseph, III, 38, 171
Pico de Gallo Salsa, 174
Pies
 Chocolate Cream Pie, 210
 Lemon Meringue Pie, 206–7
 No-Fail Piecrust, 204–5
Pineapple
 Carrot-Banana Cake, 190
 Coleslaw with Pineapple and Dried Cherries, 163
 Pineapple Upside-Down Cake, 185
 Polynesian Basting Sauce, 103
Pinto Beans with Garlic, 175
Polenta
 Creamy Polenta, 172
 Polenta Lasagna, 136, 138
 Polenta with Sausage and Roasted Peppers, 140
Polynesian Basting Sauce, 103
Pork. See also Bacon; Ham; Sausage
 Chicken and Pork Pozole, 86–87
 Chicken Relleno, 106–7
 Chili Verde, 81
 Duck Wonton Soup, 58–60
 Grandma Milici's Spaghetti and Meatballs, 128–29
 Home-Style Jook, 61
 Junkyard Dog Champion Chili, 78–79
 Kalua Pig, 70
 Matt's Sauerkraut Sausage Surprise, 88

Mom's Tamales, 74, 77
Orange and Ginger Grilled Pork Tenderloin, 65
Pork Mole, 72–73
Slow-Roasted Baby Back Ribs, 68
Potatoes
 Caldo de Res, 53
 Iron Skillet Scalloped Potatoes, 166
 Matt's Sauerkraut Sausage Surprise, 88
 Potato Fonteca, 165
 Roasted-Garlic and Sour Cream Mashed Potatoes, 170
 Three-Potato Salad, 167
 Tortilla Española, 168
 Twice-Baked Potatoes, 171
Pot Roast with Red Sauce, 66
Pozole, Chicken and Pork, 86–87
Prawns. See also Shrimp
 Firehouse 11 Cioppino, 120
 Kung Pao Prawns, 124
 Red Gumbo, 82–83
 Risotto with Prawns, 143
 Villa Gumbo, 84
Prosciutto-Wrapped Asparagus, 160
Pumpkin seeds, toasting, 43

Q
Quick Quiche with Spinach, Ham, and Mushrooms, 151

R
Raspberry Balsamic Vinaigrette, 51
Red Gumbo, 82–83
Ribs
 Grandma Milici's Spaghetti and Meatballs, 128–29
 Slow-Roasted Baby Back Ribs, 68
Rice
 Chicken Giovacchini, 110–11
 Chicken Relleno, 106–7
 Home-Style Jook, 61
 Mexican Red Rice, 174
 Risotto with Prawns, 143
 Skillet Paella, 90
 Stanyan Street Fried Rice, 173

Rigatoni alla Carbonara, 135
Risotto with Prawns, 143
Rivieccio, Claudio, 135
Roasted Asparagus with Tarragon, 158
Roasted Beet Salad with Raspberry Balsamic Vinaigrette, 51
Roasted-Garlic and Sour Cream Mashed Potatoes, 170
Rolls, Tuscan, 178
Rosemary-Garlic Roast Chicken, 108

S
Sally's Salad Dressing, 38
Salmon
 Baked Salmon Fillet with a Potato Chip Crust, 119
 Green Curry Salmon, 122
 Whole Roasted Salmon with Lemon-Basil Teriyaki, 117
Salsa, Pico de Gallo, 174
San Francisco Chocolate Chip Cookies, 212
Sauerkraut Sausage Surprise, Matt's, 88
Sausage
 Chicken and Chorizo Enchiladas, 104–5
 Chicken Relleno, 106–7
 Grandma Milici's Spaghetti and Meatballs, 128–29
 Junkyard Dog Champion Chili, 78–79
 Matt's Sauerkraut Sausage Surprise, 88
 Polenta with Sausage and Roasted Peppers, 140
 Red Gumbo, 82–83
 Skillet Paella, 90
 Swoop Stew, 71
 Tamale Pie, 85
 Turkey Meatloaf, 113
 Villa Gumbo, 84
Saxton, Sally, 38
Secret Sauce, 115
Serpa, Tony, 41
Sesame seeds, toasting, 173
Seyler, Jeanne, 119
Shrimp. See also Prawns
 Stuffed Sole Fillets, 121
 Tim's Louis Salad, 48–49

Skillet Paella, 90
Slow-Roasted Baby Back Ribs, 68
Slug Salad, 34
"Smoke and Fire" Black Beans, 176
Sole Fillets, Stuffed, 121
"Something Different" Salad, 37
Spice Rub, 68
Spicy Green Beans with Bacon, 155
Spinach
    Baked Egg Baskets, 148–50
    Joe's Special, 147
    Quick Quiche with Spinach, Ham,
        and Mushrooms, 151
    Spinach and Mushroom Sauté, 161
    Stuffed Sole Fillets, 121
Stanyan Street Fried Rice, 173
Stark, Richard V., 121
Steve's Balsamic Vinaigrette, 37
Strawberry Shortcake for a Crowd, 195–96
Stuffed Sole Fillets, 121
Swoop Stew, 71

T

Tacos, Pacific Fish, 115–16
Tamale Pie, 85
Tamales, Mom's, 74, 77
Tangy Lemon Bars, 208
Taormina, Sal, 45
Tarlach, Matt, 88
Tartar Sauce, Ed's, 103
Thai BBQ Chicken with Peanut
    Sauce, 96–97
Thai Coconut Chicken, 112
Three-Potato Salad, 167
Tim's Louis Salad, 48–49
Tin, Mike, 96
Tiramisù, 211
Tomatillos
Chili Verde, 81
Tomatoes
    Baked Egg Baskets, 148–50
    Beef Barley Soup, 55
    Caldo de Res, 53
    Fireboat BBQ Sauce, 102
    Firehouse 11 Cioppino, 120

Grandma Milici's Spaghetti and
    Meatballs, 128–29
Junkyard Dog Champion Chili, 78–79
Marinara Sauce, 136
Mexican Chicken Salad, 42
Mexican Red Rice, 174
Oxtail Ossobuco, 67
Pasta Puttanesca, 130
Penne with Chicken and Artichokes, 139
Pico de Gallo Salsa, 174
Polenta Lasagna, 136, 138
Pot Roast with Red Sauce, 66
Red Gumbo, 82–83
Risotto with Prawns, 143
Skillet Paella, 90
"Something Different" Salad, 37
Stuffed Sole Fillets, 121
Swoop Stew, 71
Tamale Pie, 85
Tim's Louis Salad, 48–49
Tomato Mozzarella Salad, 33
Tortilla Soup, 56
Villa Gumbo, 84
Tortilla Española, 168
Tortillas
    Chicken and Chorizo Enchiladas, 104–5
    Pacific Fish Tacos, 115–16
    Tortilla Soup, 56
    warming, 73
Traditions, 22–23
Triplitt, Cantrez, 106
Turkey Meatloaf, 113
Tuscan Rolls, 178
Twice-Baked Potatoes, 171

V

Velo, Jose Luis, 168
Verant, Don, 156
Verhaeg, Marty, 42, 56, 68, 113, 161, 163
Vigil, Robert, 197
Villa Gumbo, 84

W

Wagner, Rich, 122, 166

Walnuts
    Apple Walnut Crisp, 209
    Walnut Biscotti, 214
Warm Chocolate Sauce, 193
Warm Swiss Almond Apple Cake, 189
Watches, 14
Whole Roasted Salmon with Lemon-Basil
    Teriyaki, 117
Wickliffe, Bill, 102
Williams, Christine, 102
Wilson, Chase, 13, 43, 112
Wolowic, Theresa, 72
Women firefighters, 24, 137
Wonton Soup, Duck, 58–60
Woo, Terry, 36

Y

Yee, Alison, 33, 130, 214
Yucatán Marinade, 101

Z

Zammarchi, Larry, 164
Zucchini
    Polenta Lasagna, 136, 138
    Zucchini Bread, 203

MENU PLANNER

Starters
Calamari Salad, 41
Dungeness Crab Cakes, 127
Firehouse Caesar Salad, 46
"Mexican Restaurant" Salad, 43
Mixed Greens with Pears and Dried Cranberries, 52
Prosciutto-Wrapped Asparagus, 160
Roasted Beet Salad with Raspberry Balsamic Vinaigrette, 51
Slug Salad, 34
"Something Different" Salad, 37
Tomato Mozzarella Salad, 33

Potatoes, Grains, and Legumes
Creamy Polenta, 172
Iron Skillet Scalloped Potatoes, 166
Jalapeño Green Bean Delight, 156
Mexican Red Rice, 174
Pinto Beans with Garlic, 175
Potatoes Fonteca, 165
Roasted-Garlic and Sour Cream Mashed Potatoes, 170
"Smoke and Fire" Black Beans, 176
Spicy Green Beans with Bacon, 155
Stanyan Street Fried Rice, 173
Three-Potato Salad, 167
Tortilla Española, 168
Twice-Baked Potatoes, 171

Salads and Dressings
Buttermilk Ranch Dressing, 39
Calamari Salad, 41
Chinese Chicken Salad, 36
Coleslaw with Pineapple and Dried Cherries, 163
Firehouse Caesar Salad, 46
Honey-Dill Vinaigrette, 38
Mexican Chicken Salad, 42
"Mexican Restaurant" Salad, 43
Mixed Greens with Pears and Dried Cranberries, 52
Napa Cabbage Salad, 164
Roasted Beet Salad with Raspberry Balsamic
    Vinaigrette, 51
Sally's Salad Dressing, 38
Slug Salad, 34
"Something Different" Salad, 37
Three-Potato Salad, 167

Tim's Louis Salad, 48–49
Tomato Mozzarella Salad, 33

Vegetables
Dude's Ginger Carrots, 157
Jalapeño Green Bean Delight, 156
Prosciutto-Wrapped Asparagus, 160
Roasted Asparagus with Tarragon, 158
Spicy Green Beans with Bacon, 155
Spinach and Mushroom Sauté, 161

Soups
Beef Barley Soup, 55
Caldo de Res, 53
Duck Wonton Soup, 58–60
Home-Style Jook, 61
Tortilla Soup, 56

Egg Dishes
Baked Egg Baskets, 148–50
Joe's Special, 147
Quick Quiche with Spinach, Ham, and Mushrooms, 151
Tortilla Española, 168

Meat Dishes
C-Watch Fried Mein with Oyster Sauce Beef, 132–133
Grandma Milici's Spaghetti and Meatballs, 128–29
Kalua Pig, 70
Matt's Sauerkraut Sausage Surprise, 88
Mom's Tamales, 74, 77
Orange and Ginger Grilled Pork Tenderloin, 65
Oxtail Ossobuco, 67
Pot Roast with Red Sauce, 66
Slow-Roasted Baby Back Ribs, 68
Tamale Pie, 85

Pasta, Rice, and Polenta
Creamy Polenta, 172
C-Watch Fried Mein with Oyster Sauce Beef, 132–133
Grandma Milici's Spaghetti and Meatballs, 128–29
Mexican Red Rice, 174
Pasta Puttanesca, 130
Penne with Chicken and Artichokes, 139
Polenta Lasagna, 136, 138
Polenta with Sausage and Roasted Peppers, 140
Rigatoni alla Carbonara, 135

Risotto with Prawns, 143
Skillet Paella, 90

Stews
California Chicken Adobo, 91
Chicken and Pork Pozole, 86–87
Chili Verde, 81
Firehouse 11 Cioppino, 120
Junkyard Dog Champion Chili, 78–79
Pork Mole, 72–73
Red Gumbo, 82–83
Stanyan Street Fried Rice, 173
Swoop Stew, 71
Villa Gumbo, 84

Poultry Dishes
Bob's Oven-Fried Chicken, 95
Buz's Perfect Fried Chicken, 94
California Chicken Adobo, 91
Chicken and Chorizo Enchiladas, 104–5
Chicken Giovacchini, 110–11
Chicken in a Barrel, 92–93
Chicken Relleno, 106–7
Chinese Chicken Salad, 36
Mexican Chicken Salad, 42
Rosemary-Garlic Roast Chicken, 108
Thai BBQ Chicken with Peanut Sauce, 96–97
Thai Coconut Chicken, 112
Turkey Meatloaf, 113

Seafood Dishes
Baked Salmon Fillet with a Potato Chip Crust, 119
Blackened Red Snapper, 126
Calamari Salad, 41
Dungeness Crab Cakes, 127
Firehouse 11 Cioppino, 120
Green Curry Salmon, 122
Kung Pao Prawns, 124
Pacific Fish Tacos, 115–16
Stuffed Sole Fillets, 121
Tim's Louis Salad, 48–49
Whole Roasted Salmon with Lemon-Basil Teriyaki, 117

Main Dishes for a Crowd
Grandma Milici's Spaghetti and Meatballs, 128–29
Junkyard Dog Champion Chili, 78–79
Matt's Sauerkraut Sausage Surprise, 88

Red Gumbo, 82–83
Skillet Paella, 90
Tamale Pie, 85
Villa Gumbo, 84

Meatless Main Dishes
Artichoke and Mushroom Focaccia, 144
Polenta Lasagna, 136, 138

Marinades and Sauces
"Any Kind of Meat" Marinade, 101
Ed's Tartar Sauce, 103
Fireboat BBQ Sauce, 102
Honey-Mustard Marinade, 102
Pico de Gallo Salsa, 174
Polynesian Basting Sauce, 103
Yucatán Marinade, 101

Breads
Artichoke and Mushroom Focaccia, 144
Green Chile and Cheese Cornbread, 181
Irish Soda Bread, 177
Tuscan Rolls, 178
Zucchini Bread, 203

Desserts
Apple Walnut Crisp, 209
Applesauce Fruitcake, 187
Brown Sugar-Berry Coffee Cake, 201
Carrot-Banana Cake, 190
Chocolate Chip Cheesecake, 197
Chocolate Cream Pie, 210
Crazy Cake, 198
Five-Minute "Free Cake," 200
Lemon Meringue Pie, 206–7
Lemon Milk Cake, 186
Lemon Pound Cake, 192
No-Fail Piecrust, 204–5
Pineapple Upside-Down Cake, 185
San Francisco Chocolate Chip Cookies, 212
Strawberry Shortcake for a Crowd, 195–96
Tangy Lemon Bars, 208
Tiramisù, 211
Walnut Biscotti, 214
Warm Chocolate Sauce, 193
Warm Swiss Almond Apple Cake, 189
Zucchini Bread, 203

TABLE OF EQUIVALENTS

The exact equivalents in the following tables have been rounded for convenience.

Liquid/Dry Measures

U.S.	METRIC
1/4 teaspoon	1.25 milliliters
1/2 teaspoon	2.5 milliliters
1 teaspoon	5 milliliters
1 tablespoon (3 teaspoons)	15 milliliters
1 fluid ounce (2 tablespoons)	30 milliliters
1/4 cup	60 milliliters
1/3 cup	80 milliliters
1/2 cup	120 milliliters
1 cup	240 milliliters
1 pint (2 cups)	480 milliliters
1 quart (4 cups; 32 ounces)	960 milliliters
1 gallon (4 quarts)	3.84 liters
1 ounce (by weight)	28 grams
1 pound	454 grams
2.2 pounds	1 kilogram

Length Measures

U.S.	METRIC
1/8 inch	3 millimeters
1/4 inch	6 millimeters
1/2 inch	12 millimeters
1 inch	2.5 centimeters

Oven Temperatures

FAHRENHEIT	CELSIUS	GAS
250	120	1/2
275	140	1
300	150	2
325	160	3
350	180	4
375	190	5
400	200	6
425	220	7
450	230	8
475	240	9
500	260	10